BUTT NAKED LEADERSHIP

HAVING THE COURAGE TO DISCOVER YOUR
PURPOSE AND LIVE OUT YOUR DESTINY
WITH CONFIDENCE

SONIA HASSEY

DEDICATION

This book is dedicated to my daughters, Yesenia and Hannah.

TABLE OF CONTENTS

CHAPTER 1

The Making Of A Leader

———⁓⁓⁓———

Everyone on this planet is born with a purpose. Each of us has been sealed with it since birth. Unfortunately, many people go through life without knowing their purpose, and they live their lives by default instead of by deliberate design. Once we get clear on our purpose and what we desire, we can design our lives. This is definitely not an easy process. In our fast-paced world with demands pulling us in all directions, we need to intentionally pause and reflect on our lives and the things that matter. We need to ask ourselves deep questions.

If you had one year to live, how would you spend your life? What impact would you choose to make, and what priorities would you set? What habits would you stop doing that are not serving you, and what habits would you start? These are important questions that you need to ask yourself. Getting to know yourself takes time; it's about purposefully going deep into your core and discovering your true identity.

For many years, I lived my life as it came to me. My marriage, my children, my job and my daily routine made for a so-called normal life. As the years went by, I realized how empty I truly was. My life seemed perfect on the outside and it wasn't anything to complain about; however, deep down inside I wasn't living my true identity. I felt like a shell with no emotion, just living life and trying to please people. I tried to live my life as perfectly as I knew how, but I felt a hole that I couldn't fill.

As my burden became evident to me, I began to pray about this emptiness. At this point, I couldn't ignore how I was feeling. I realized that I had to figure my life out, but at the same time, it also scared me that I had no idea what I was going to dig up out of my deep longing for something real. I soon realized that this was a defining moment in my life. An awakening was stirring up in me and I wasn't quite sure how to deal with it. I also knew that there was no turning back, and I felt a paradigm shifting.

This was the beginning of discovering my true identity. It was me finally paying attention to the missing piece of my life: what my purpose was in this crazy world and how I fit into it. I soon realized that going through the motions and living a routine life until I die was not the ideal life that I wanted to live. I knew that I was created for so much more. Once I realized this awareness for myself, I began to dig deeper into the empty space and figure out why I was empty. I began to ask myself why I felt this way; then more questions snowballed from there. Wow! To my amazement, for the first time, I realized how much my life needed to make sense to me. My daily prayers were asking God for my real purpose.

I set the intention to read many books on self-development. A new world of possibilities started opening up in my mind, and to my amazement, for the first time, I started searching for all the things that I was passionate about. It was like looking through a lens that was finally at its perfect focus, and it was a view of everything that I loved.

As a hairstylist, I realized how much I loved to encourage and empower people to make changes in their lives for the better. It fulfilled me as I was in deep conversations with my clients. I have vivid memories of very empowering moments with my clients. One in particular was a young woman who was going to school to become a nurse, and she told me that she wanted to become a nurse because that's what her family expected of her. However, she wasn't truly fulfilled, and by the time we ended our lengthy conversation, she realized her passion was to be healthy and fit and she wanted to inspire others to also be health conscious as well. She began to do research right from her phone, and take immediate action on her goals to become a Health Coach, and now she is fulfilling her passion. I cannot begin to tell you what that does to me when someone gets a paradigm shift right before my eyes! Boom! It's like magic to see one's real journey begin.

Another example was a young man in his third year of college. He began to tell me that he had been going to college for three years and still didn't know what he wanted to do as a career. He said that he was in college because his parents told him that he had to go. It's crazy to believe that people can go to college and spend tons of money, and most likely get deep into debt with student loans, yet with no direction in mind. Well, that was the case with this young man. I began to talk with him about his passions and the gifts that come naturally to him. Something clicked with this young man, and he literally told me that he was going to talk to his parents and tell them that he was going to quit spending their money on college so that he could pursue what he really wanted to do. Wow! I felt like he wanted to just jump out of the chair and run to his parents to let them know. I never heard from him again, but I feel for sure that he is on the right track and fulfilling his true purpose.

These are two of many powerful stories that have occurred from my hairstyling chair. They are part of a collection of magical moments for me, I must say! As I began to ponder all the years of enjoying these great awakening conversations with clients, I began to see my own passion a lot clearer. Soon after I myself came to my own awakening, I began to search out how I could leverage my skills to help many more people. This is when I realized that becoming a certified Life Coach would be a great fit for me. I realized that this career would help me improve many people's lives for the better.

One of the most important things we can do is to stop and listen to that true voice inside each of us. Unfortunately, many people don't take the time to listen and discover themselves in a deeper way.

It's that small voice that wants to reveal your true purpose. You were born for a specific purpose, and it's not something you search for: It's within you. Your true abundant life is waiting to be discovered. If there's a void in your life and you can't figure out what it is, as I experienced, then that is your signal to discover what that void is. It's like when you have pain in your body, or a simple headache, you know that something is going on that is giving you those symptoms. When you feel a void, you know something so much greater than you is calling you out and searching for the treasure in your soul. Keep searching until you find it, because it is right there. And when you find it, it's like an explosion of fireworks that just occurs inside of you and you know that you will never be the same again. Then, it's all about putting the pieces together. That takes a lot of thinking and work, but with this new fuel of passion added to the puzzle, you will seek your new journey more diligently!

You contain three key ingredients: passion, energy and purpose. When you find your purpose, you will connect it with your passion, and fire it up with energy!

Simon Sinek suggests the following questions to help you discover your voice; your divine purpose: What's your purpose? What's your cause? What's your belief? Why does your business exist? Why do you get out of bed every morning? Why should anyone care? These important questions should give you a kick-start. Take your time answering them. These questions take deep thought. Begin to write down all your answers, and you'll be surprised to see what's deep inside your heart. You can also ask people close to you to describe your gifts. Make this an intentional journey. Discover as much about you as possible. Discover your strengths: the skills that you are good at. My team and I took the StrengthsFinder test by Tom Rath, and I was amazed at its accuracy. I highly recommend it if you are not sure about your strengths.

I can honestly tell you that I was not fulfilled until I finally understood my true identity and began to live it out. Yes! As you can see, it takes a lot of soul-searching to know yourself at your core. It is vital for us to understand that we must understand ourselves and know our voices before we can truly lead others. This discovery is the most profound action you can take for yourself and for others, because you will be giving the world the real gift of you! The two most important days of your life will be the day you were born, and the day you discovered why. Having a clear self-discovery will prepare you for your leadership journey.

On the contrary, if you don't fully understand your voice or you are not truly centered, you will pull on your heart or emotions. This can leave room for many unintentional hurtful situations impacting people in negative ways. Know what you want, how you want to lead and what impact you want to have as a leader. Your impact will have a ripple effect in a positive or negative way. From the moment you decide to lead, be intentional with people in every situation, as they will shape your character, and you will shape theirs. As a heart-driven leader, character will be your rudder. Character will guide you and protect you.

Being true to yourself is a personal choice for truth. It means making choices about how you want to live. You have the total power to live your life any way you want and to be faithful to the truth about you. It means you don't worry about pleasing other people; living by someone else's standards or rules. You don't care what people think of you. You live as your natural self. Without compromise. No one can tell you how to be true to yourself except you.

Whatever you do, don't beat yourself up, don't berate yourself, and don't forget that it takes courage to be true to who you are in a world that is in such a hurry to measure you up and judge you at every turn. But also know this: You have the courage. Deep down, you can muster the courage to be your true self if you make up your mind to do so.

When you are true to yourself, you allow your individuality and uniqueness to shine through. You respect the opinions of others but do not conform to stereotypes or their expectations of you. Being true to yourself is what your heart and soul yearn for. Being true to yourself is the only way to achieve inner peace. It sets you free and floods you with joy and fulfillment.

If given the choice, you would not want to abandon your true self to be someone else – you would feel lost and confused being anyone else but yourself and who you were meant to be – no matter how wealthy, how "lucky" or how popular the "fake" you may be. Of course, you do have the choice! So why would you want to bet your happiness on something you can never have? Would you want to give up your own abundance for an empty desire?

According to David Wolfe, trying to be someone you're not is a battle between your head and your heart. Your head may be making the decisions, but all the while, your heart is feeling the pain of having to mask your true self. If your heart isn't into it, whatever it is, chances are that it's not right for you. Learn to listen to your heart and let it lead you. Trust your instincts and have faith in yourself. Self-love is the first step to becoming comfortable in your own skin.

Be true to the very best that is in you and live your life consistent with your highest values and aspirations. Those who are most successful in life have dared to creatively express themselves, and in turn, broaden the experiences and perspectives of everyone else around them.

This is the greatest gift I have given myself: to be the most authentic me that I can be, and to express it. One thing I know about myself is that I am a passionate person. When I have a conviction about something and really want to express myself, my passion comes across in my body language and voice. Before I began working on my own self-development, I realized that I expressed myself in this way, and I felt embarrassed afterward. I felt like it was a bit too much for people, but a friend told me that it is who I am and that's why people are inspired. I know that when I am sharing, it truly comes from my heart, and now I realize that it is simply me and all of me. I can't change who I am and I have now learned to embrace my personality. It is the greatest feeling ever to be comfortable in your own skin. It is freeing, to say the least.

One of the greatest challenges, as we journey to discover our divine purposes and set our goals, is to realize that life still has its trouble spots. And these challenges will test our true identities and our characters. The choices we make on a daily basis will question who we really are. We can know our purpose and still decide to make the wrong choices. We must have the courage to walk the journey that is set before us, to stay true to ourselves and keep steering in the right direction. We can be tempted to take shortcuts. We need to be careful and let peace guide the way, and know that success is in the journey. We need to be present and future-focused, understanding that all we have is today and we must make the best of today, while at the same time taking action steps to our goals every day. Living a purpose-driven life is exactly that: living on purpose every single day. We wake up knowing exactly what our plans are for the day.

I never take for granted the opportunity to work on myself daily. I can't say that I'm faithful 100 percent of the time, but I make the effort every day to listen to audios, work on my affirmations and learn more about my field of work. We have to get better at what we do, and we can always grow through self-development. Know what you want and where you want to go at all times. Lead yourself in such a way that you know what works for you and what doesn't work, and then it will be incredibly impactful when you lead others. Lead others in the way that you would want to be led; this is the key to your leadership role and your relationships.

Questions to ask yourself:

1. If you had one year to live, how would you live it?

2. Do you know your life purpose? If yes, what is it?

3. Do you believe in a particular cause?

4. Are you being true to yourself personally and as a leader?

CHAPTER 2

From Faint To Spark

———⁂———

How wrong I was to think that living a life that looked great from the outside with a normal daily routine would be the perfect life for me. As we all know, that lifestyle never brings complete satisfaction. Everyone has a deep longing for meaning and purpose. The worst part about living the so-called perfect life was that I was pretending to be fine, when I actually felt miserable inside.

The more I talked with people, the more I realized how many others were living a normal life without passion because they were not living the abundant life that they were destined to live. It's like living as a shell, and you don't know what's on the inside. And it causes deep insecurity, emptiness and pain, while trying to figure out what is really going on.

My first realization was that I was unhappy and wanted to discover how to truly be happy. Soon after, I began to think about the things that I wanted out of life. My self-discovery was happening right before my eyes – and boom! This is when it all began. It sounds silly now, but this was truly the beginning of my new journey. It was important for me to understand where I was at the time and where I wanted to be. I had to pause and dig deep into my heart to figure out my destiny and what I wanted from myself. What followed was more desire and small action steps toward discovering myself. Dreams and visions inspired more curiosity about my true identity. I couldn't help but start to feel an awakening in my spirit; a small burst of excitement.

When my oldest daughter was 16 years old, I would take her to the youth group at our local church, and I enjoyed watching the youth get inspired, desire a heart for God and seek meaning in their lives. Something gripped my heart, seeing them seek for what's real. I remember every week for months, sitting way in the back and just observing, until one day I realized that I wanted to help them in some way. I started pondering the idea that I could make a difference in their lives. This went on for about a year before I took action. I finally built up the courage to talk to the youth pastor and ask him if I could serve the youth in any way. I got excited, and at the same time, I was scared to death because I had no idea what I was getting into. He realized I was eager to jump in.

At this time in my life, I was not secure in my identity and for sure didn't have much confidence, but this desire to keep searching kept getting stronger to the point where I was thinking about it all the time. The funny part about finally talking to someone (the youth pastor) about my desire to help in some way is that I was asked to start passing out pencils. I couldn't believe it! But I still didn't know how I wanted to help, so I just kept going and helping out with small stuff. After a few months, I felt a strong desire to do something greater. Inside, I wanted to teach the youth something.

Then one day, I built up the courage to go to the youth pastor again and ask him if I could teach the youth. He had seen my desire and faithfulness throughout the months, and immediately said yes! Soon after, we went to a youth conference where it all became real to me, and I realized that I could have an impact on young people. At the conference, he bought workbooks for me, and at that moment I realized that it was all happening. I said to myself, "Okay I can do this!" But then fear crept in and said, "You have never taught before, so how are you going to do this?" Aww! The crazy emotional roller coaster that followed wouldn't stop.

I totally get it now: how many people stop at this point in fulfilling their dreams. We have to cross over so many hurdles in our minds. No one has ever said that stepping out of our comfort zones was going to be easy, but it's important to take mini-steps toward our goals every day until we reach them. Any time we step out of our comfort zones, there will always be some sort of fear creeping in;

however, it should never paralyze us. If it does, we have to realize what is hindering us and work on it until it is removed.

It's valuable to get help from a counselor or a coach to help us get through the mental sabotage. The mindset is very powerful! According to Napoleon Hill, we become what we think about all day long. Fear, doubt and unbelief are not what we want to linger on the forefront of our mindsets every waking hour, as they will keep us in a place of uncertainty and lack. That is how I lived for so many years, and now I realize what a waste of time it was. I'm beyond grateful that I had the deepest hunger to desire what life has to offer, even though I didn't know exactly what it would look like. I just kept going until it became clear and I realized my vision and destiny for my life.

Within one month of talking to the pastor about wanting to teach the youth, I found myself in a class with 15 youth who were leaders. My job was to help them believe in their destinies and take action on them, and to have faith that their destinies would come to pass. I'm telling you, I truly was scared to death, yet it was exhilarating at the same time. I literally prayed and studied every day in preparation. It was to be a two-hour class and I had to make sure I had content for the whole time. Even if you've never worked with youth, you probably know they get bored easily, and it shows. Trust me! I was on my toes all the time, making sure that I had good content and could keep them engaged.

I taught this "Battle Cry" class for four years straight every Sunday, and unbeknownst to me at the time, it was a great success! Students in my class were transformed personally and spiritually. Some are doing great things right now. One created a nationwide movement. He believed in his destiny and pushed through all the obstacles, and is now sharing stages with worldwide leaders. This is just one example of the impact that Battle Cry had on the youth, and on me. I matured in so many areas of my life. I will never forget this experience, as it was my humble beginnings to my own destiny. This is where I learned that speaking and teaching were my gifts. I never would've known if I didn't just jump in, even though I had no idea what I was doing at the start.

Being a hairstylist for over 30 years also showed me that I could empower people to become more, and help them realize their destinies and learn how to get unstuck in their lives – and this was another huge sign about my own purpose.

After the Battle Cry class ended four years later, I realized that I still had so much to learn. A lot of my teaching came from reading scripture and exploring my faith. I now was hungry to learn more about teaching and mentoring, and I also realized that learning more about myself and studying self-development would be my next big steps.

I met another pastor who told me he would mentor me if I would go to the Philippines with him and his wife. I jumped on the opportunity, and two weeks later, I was on a plane with two strangers. It felt right and I knew that it was going to change my life, Sure enough, it did! I came back a different person; I was awakened to new possibilities. It was like a whole new world was opened up to me! When I returned, I bought books and began to read like it was food for my soul. I just couldn't stop reading. I was in my own little world with new desires that I had never experienced before. I also began to go to conferences to listen to motivational speakers. I found myself traveling to other states to listen to the greats about transformation and business development. I was on my own quest to fulfill the desires that were deep inside of me.

After a full year of reading and traveling, I realized that I wanted to become a certified Life Coach. I knew it was a good fit because it would leverage my interest in speaking to audiences and working one-on-one with people. So, here I went again. I headed to Texas for a week to get certified. I felt like it was a great accomplishment, but when I returned, I didn't quite know what to do with my certification, or how to begin.

Oh, this crazy journey! Just when I thought I was going to land and it would all come to me, I realized that's not how it was working out at all. I felt like I was back to ground zero, trying to figure out how to begin my new journey again. I literally was clueless. So, I returned from my Life Coach certification and went back to the salon and started working on hair as usual. Weeks and months went by, and not knowing what my next step should be, I felt like I was stopped in my tracks. It's interesting how we can easily go back to the old routine once we stop taking the initiative to move forward; that's exactly what I did.

After a few months, one of my clients asked me to go to a business group that met every Wednesday morning. He said it would be great to expose myself more as a hairstylist. I thought, "Well, why not?" So I went to the meeting and I introduced myself as a hairstylist and told them a little bit about me. It felt weird because I felt like I jumped back to the person I had been for years, and it was just all too easy to be the old me. I joined this networking group, and the people were nice and it was in a small community where everyone knew each other. It felt good to just belong to a group of people who wanted to move their businesses forward.

The dream of doing something that was beyond me was still creeping up on me daily. It was always on my mind, but the realist in me settled deep and thought, "Well, one day I will run into my dream and it will all happen, just like that!" One day, after about a year of going to the business networking meetings, the president of the group asked me in front of everyone if I had ever thought about running a women's group in town. I thought to myself, "What did he just say?" The moment he spoke those words, I knew that I had to look into this and understand how it could work. Crazy to think, just like that, the fire in me would begin to burn into flames again. It all happened in a moment. I have read in Ecclesiastes that time and chance happen to everyone, and I truly felt at that moment that this the moment it was happening for me.

The president of the men's club was also in this group, and I immediately asked him how he got started, and we set a date to meet for coffee the following week. I'll never forget; it was a Monday morning. I brought two friends and he brought someone from the Chamber and the newspaper, which was interesting because I had no idea that we were going to have a meeting with six people. He began to tell me how simple it was to get started, and how I could create my own group easily. I thought, "Wow! I can really do this!" I began to get excited about it and I felt like my life was going to change in an instant. And sure enough, all of them asked if I would start the women's group in town. Without hesitation, I said yes! I told them it felt like I was jumping into a pool and I had no idea how deep it was. The unknown! They all smiled and said, "Great! When would you like to start?" I said, "I'm not quite sure yet." Then the newspaper lady said, "If you would like to start later this week, I can put it in the paper by tomorrow." I said, "What? That soon? Wait! I need to have an idea of what this looks like, and I'm not quite sure yet." They all immediately said that they would help me get it started. I took a deep breath and said "Yes! Let's do this!" I knew that if I didn't do it right then, then when would I build up the courage to do it?

Literally two days later, I created the "Women Inspired Network." The time and place were in the paper, and 15 women showed up. My first talk was about the mission of the network. I put together the core values, and the group took off from there! It was an amazing launch and many women were attracted to it. We built a strong team and met every week. We decided to become a strong alliance for our community. We regularly created events and gave back to local nonprofits that were in need. The women said they felt fulfilled as they knew they were giving back in such a meaningful way. Our community was small, so it became personal for everyone. We also created a strong team and sisterhood, and we challenged one another and collaborated to make these events successful. I cannot even describe the feeling of accomplishment that I felt. A powerful force of network, to say the least.

We became well-known in the community and were in the newspaper almost every week. We got involved in parades and other activities in town. We created something that had meaning and purpose. But one year into this amazing heart of giving back, I also saw somewhat of a breakdown with the women. I knew that as women, we can multitask and succeed in many ways; however, I started to see their weariness. I found myself constantly encouraging them, but it wasn't enough. I honestly felt like there was a shift in their interest and love for giving.

I remember going home one day after a meeting and putting thought into this concern of mine. I prayed and asked, "What can I do to shift this?" I knew that something had to change soon, or I was going to lose them. Weeks went by and nothing changed. During this time, I was in the process of turning this network into a nonprofit, but I also wasn't feeling peaceful about it, and now I began to struggle with the idea because I had the women in mind. I knew that I had to do something for them; not just ask them to serve others 100 percent of the time. I began to think about how I could empower them so they could become better and give more, as they desired. Then it hit me! I thought, "Why don't I create a weekly program so we can learn and share about ourselves?" We began with a book club, then I brought in speakers on personal-development subjects, and I started to speak and coach the group as well. Meanwhile, we continued with our events to serve the community. I put together a monthly program, and it was working,

I then realized that this was my true calling: empowering women to do and be their best, so they can give their best to the world around them. Soon after, women visited our group from other cities. That was refreshing, and I saw the paradigm shift in the network happen right before my eyes. It was pretty amazing to see it unfold.

This was when I realized that I did not want the network to be a nonprofit after all, and at the same time, I knew that this decision would stir things up with some women in the community. As far as the community was concerned, our involvement wasn't going to change. The change would come with empowering the women with the right tools so they would stay in their areas of strength and believe that they could accomplish whatever they confidently set their minds to accomplish. I wanted to build the women from the inside out. I planned for the new business to become a monthly membership with a cost. I knew that I had to deliver the vision, and I also knew that the cost would take it to a different level in so many positive ways.

As I prepared to share the new plan and vision with the women, I was nervous because I had no idea what the outcome would be. I stood up and shared with them, and asked if they had any questions. As I was speaking, I could tell that some were not agreeing with the new idea. I had made up my mind that this was ultimately what I was supposed to create, and I was ready for pushback. And sure enough, some women walked out, and some emailed me and told me that it wasn't going to work for them. My heart sank, but I reminded myself that I was expecting this to happen and that it would get better from here. Some of the women stayed and supported the idea. It took months before things were smooth again, and I just trusted the process and kept innovating.

Even though we were still supporting and bringing funds to the community, the newspaper lady called me and told me that they would no longer promote the group since it was not a nonprofit. It literally broke my heart. I remember just dropping everything and crying my eyes out. I felt like the whole town let me down after we had given so much to the community. However, it was interesting to me how serving the community wouldn't change in any way, and the only thing that would change would be the extra service I was providing for these women. It was as if the community as a whole couldn't understand the power of developing women to serve in a grander way. I knew that I had to stick to what I truly believed was the right thing to do.

Sure enough, it became a success after a few months, and I have never regretted any of the changes. My team had a lot of synergy, and we had so much fun! I now realize even more how the journey can get bumpy along the way, but we have to trust the process, no matter what! Believe in your purpose so much so that it is strong, and no one, or nothing, will stand in its way. Believe and it will get accomplished.

For two years I was in the small town of Galt, California. The town where it all began for me; I will never forget that. Then the next powerful and scary shift happened around the two-year mark of being in business, and I felt like it was time to move on to another city. I began to dream bigger and wanted to bring more women into the network who understood my vision and believed in the power of personal development. I began going to other networking events and meeting great people who also encouraged me to expand to a bigger city. I had no idea how my present group was going to react to the sudden change; however, I spoke to them about the big vision for all of us. A few on our team were ready to join me in bringing our group to a bigger city. I knew it was my next step!

I rented a co-working space and began my events in Sacramento, 30 miles north of Galt. Only this time, it was all about empowering women, and I didn't feel ready to start giving back to another community with such a small team. I needed to build a new team and start fresh again, and I also knew that I wanted to empower women more than ever! I wanted to create a unique network that would change women's lives forever. This passion ran deep. I knew that it was going to look completely different; I just didn't quite know exactly how yet.

I'm thankful for the people who came into my life, who encouraged me and helped me move forward. I know that no one succeeds alone. I needed the support, because here came another amazing shift in my life which took me and the business to a whole new level. One week before Christmas, I received a clear vision that I will never forget. I truly believe it was a vision from God. I saw myself in a conference room with about 20 women and I was wearing a black skirt and a white top, and my hair was in a bun. I know, it's kinda funny when I think about it, but it was so vivid and the impression that it gave me was very powerful! I saw myself speaking to the women with such a powerful voice, and what came to me was that I would be speaking life to them, and whatever I spoke to them would come to pass. And there it was! A beautiful vision of what would come to pass in my business. I just knew it! There was no doubt in me at all about what was coming next. Again, not knowing how, but I just knew that it would come to pass.

I soon told two friends, and they helped me bring this vision to reality. And sure enough, exactly one month later, the vision unfolded exactly the way I imagined. I cast a grand vision for women in leadership to help them lead their movements, whether in business, nonprofits, or ministry, so they can confidently rise up and bring significance to their lives and the lives of those they lead. I realized that my vision had grown! Now I realized that I was truly taking a huge step of faith to bring this amazing vision to pass. Well, the moment came and 20 women signed up, exactly how I saw it in the vision.

Our new leadership program is called Destiny Women Global. This is the first new leg for Women Inspired Network Inc. Now, this was exciting! It was exactly at the heart of my passion. Finally! My dream had come true! It was definitely scary for me because I knew that I had to deliver what I promised. So here I was, ready to shoot these women to the moon with their passion and success! I was all fired up and ready to give my heart and soul to my calling. We began to meet weekly and I aimed to bring these women to a new level in their leadership and personal development.

As a few months went by, I realized that most of the women needed to believe more in themselves, and they needed to be healed from past hurts. It soon became evident that I needed to shift the way I talked with these women. Instead of talking about their businesses, I needed to talk more about self-development in order for them to become great leaders. I spoke with them about the shift that had to happen for their businesses to move forward. I called it the Year of Transformation, and that's exactly what it was. This personal growth happened to all of us, including me. And I am so grateful for it! It still continues; we never stop needing to grow. I am definitely not the same person I was in the first year. We all learned many great lessons, for sure.

A year later, we called it the Year of Acceleration. Our team has truly come a long way in our leadership journeys and our businesses. So many great things are in store for Destiny Women Global. Sometimes I wonder how I will keep up, but I put everything in perspective and take action on the goals that are pressing at the moment. The most important things I learned as a leader are knowing when to make changes, listening for the next step and listening to those you lead.

I will never forget asking a successful woman to have coffee with me so I could learn from her. One of my first questions was, "When do I know when it's time for the next step in my business?" I felt like it was a good question, but she told me that she couldn't answer that question, because only in the journey will I know how to answer that question for myself. I was hoping for a better answer; however, now I fully understand what she meant.

I believe we have to be aware of the crossroads and the opportunities for our next big moves, but we can miss them if we are not watchful in the journey. I believe that so far I have made the right moves and have taken the necessary risks for myself and my business. The other important advice she gave me was to always structure my business in a way that makes sense to me and my clients. To this day, I'm grateful to her for giving me great advice.

Questions to ask yourself:

1. What action steps can you take right now that will draw you closer to your purpose?

2. What do you think is holding you back from taking action toward your goals?

3. Do you have a mentor or a coach who is guiding you to success?

4. On a scale of 1–10, how ready are you to discover your true purpose?

CHAPTER 3

The Deep Work

Now, this is the part that can make or break us as heart-driven leaders. Any time we are ready to move into new territories in our lives, fear and anxiety will creep in. Somehow, we easily convince ourselves that maybe it's not what we were supposed to do – and that is the fear talking! We back away and retreat to our comfort zones. It's the feeling of the unknown, and it's uncomfortable because we always want to know the outcome in every situation. This is the part that tries to prevent us from succeeding in anything worthwhile. We have to go into the unknown, as scary as it may seem. We have to deal with all the fears that creep in. Our desire to succeed has to be so strong that we will take that next step forward, no matter what!

I lived in this frozen comfort zone for years, while at the same time having a burning desire to speak up or to approach someone when I wanted to. Yet I was timid to the point of being frozen in my tracks. I hated myself every time I did that, and I knew that deep down inside it was hurting me. The real me was struggling to come out, step out, or speak. This battle of the mind happened for years. It drove me crazy at times! I was in a deep, dark battle in my mind that no one knew about. I remember reaching the point when I was fearing death; it's amazing where the mind can take you when you meditate on negative things all the time. In this state of mind, I wished I was someone else. The torment was real!

It now saddens me to see women suffering in their mindsets, because it completely stops them from truly living fulfilled lives. You can never discover your divine purpose in this condition. It's like a clogged-up funnel with no air to breath, no creativity, only self-sabotage and the entanglement of everything that you were created to do. You cannot think or see clearly. I am talking about real, powerful women not being able to live out their fullest potential because they are stuck in one form or another. They are well aware of their gifts and their potential, but just can't seem to move forward due to unresolved pain from the past.

I believe the first thing you have to do is ask yourself what lies you are believing about yourself. Why are you believing these lies? What is causing you to believe these untruths? Are these beliefs true about yourself? This can be a painful process; however, in order for you to realize your purpose and do great things in the world, you have to clear out all the areas where you are stuck. Healing and wholeness have to take place. If you have deep wounds as I did, you might want to consider hiring a Life Coach or a counselor. It will be worth the cost and time. There is no way you can skip this process if you have a dream that is bigger than you! Your happiness, your fulfillment and your purpose are on the line here. There is a world out there that is waiting for you to serve with the gifts that you have been given. Get restored! Show up in your uniqueness and power, so that the people who you are serving can be restored and healed as well.

I realized that getting out of my comfort zone was actually not about me; it was about serving others by using the gifts and talents that I was uniquely created to share. That's what gave me the courage to take baby steps at the beginning of my new journey to freedom.

The work is deep and hard, I cannot lie to you, but this is where real courage can be found. It's in the most vulnerable place: the place where the shame is and all the ugly stuff that no one sees except you and God. The place where we never want to visit, nor confront. You have what it takes to rise up and face the pain, and sometimes you won't fully understand what is going on with your emotions as you dig deep in that place. Keep digging; it's all there. There is a reason for your struggle. Determine to never let it have power over you again. When you realize what's really going on inside of you, you will need to take action steps. For example, forgiving people who hurt you, or forgiving yourself (sometimes that's the most difficult one), but you have to give yourself permission to forgive or you cannot fully move forward.

Every time you need to step into new territory in your life or business, you will always find some type of struggle. But it's worth it! Many women I have personally come across have completely disappeared when they realized it was time to do the inner work; they were too afraid to dig into the vulnerable place. This is where my heart bleeds for them, and this is my mission in life: to help women push through the hard and the true, so they can be reborn again and fully live out their destinies!

As for me, I came from a place of fearing people and fearing life itself, and literally hiding behind the safety of routine, to now truly loving people and desiring to get to know their uniqueness and hearing their stories. Everyone has a story and many are about transformation. Now I love life and everything it has to offer, especially the simple things. Like being in the moment, laughing, being silly, dancing and loving. These are the beautiful moments that I will never miss out on again. Being me, all me and never holding back. I'm definitely not saying that my life is perfect; however, it's the transformation that has made all the difference for me to be able to live authentically. I cannot put a price on the peace and abundance that I feel, and knowing that I am blessed and deserve to be so.

Now I wait in expectation for good to come to me, and I believe that I deserve the best that life has to offer. I get excited and enjoy every step of the journey. Having faith is also a big part of the journey because the journey is not a straight line. Part of my daily routine is to ask God for guidance through prayer. I also know that I can't speed the process in any way and that some of the deep work may take longer than anticipated. This is why faith is a vital part of the process. You have to believe that the Creator of the universe has laid out His divine purpose for your life, and you must take the necessary steps and have the patience to fully transform into your destiny.

Once you begin your journey intentionally, you will have what I call God Moments. These are when you are truly connected at the heart and your thoughts are all focused on the right things, like God, love, people, passion, community and purpose. When your heart is full of pleasant thoughts, you will experience moments of inspiration, wisdom and innovation. People will come into your mind that you miss and need to reconnect with. This area humbles me because I realize there is so much more that I can do to connect and better serve people. This is the place where I desire to be 100 percent of the time; however, busyness and not using my time wisely can steal everything that matters to me and put me in a place of scarcity and frustration. We all know it's not a good place to be, but it amazes me how easily we can lose focus if we are not intentional every day.

The real question is: How can we keep from so easily slipping back into the old routines? How can we avoid that lack of focus? Write your goals down and focus on the prize as often as you can, and do not let your mind wander into worrisome or negative areas. Stay focused on the things that bring love, harmony and gratefulness, and let your work flow with these positive thoughts. If you want a life of meaning and purpose, then your actions must connect with your heart; this is the authenticity I discussed earlier. It's also listening to the gentle nudge for your next direction, then confidently taking that path. Get away from the noise of life's demands that can reel you in over time, because before you know it, you can easily lose track. Be careful, because it can be hard to get back in motion once you've been distracted.

I love the word metanoia – a transformative change of heart. This is exactly what has to happen to everyone in order to make our world a better place. Yes, indeed! It begins with you and me. It's a great responsibility we have to our Creator and to ourselves and to each other. Consider your life as an adventure every day, find something new you are going to learn or create, and wait in expectation for great results. Whatever you sow, you will reap.

Nevertheless, love and trust the journey as it is uniquely yours. Life is truly abundant and amazing when you have this perspective. Open the curtain to your beautiful life. Do you see it? Don't be afraid; it's yours to discover, believe and create, and no one can create it the way you were meant to. I remember listening to Les Brown when he said to imagine, at the end of your life, that you are lying in bed and all your gifts and talents are surrounding you – the ones you never used – and asking you why you didn't put them to use. It's a cute image; but can you really imagine it? I can only imagine myself before God as He asks me how I used all my talents. All I want to hear is "Good job!" Now that would be the ultimate reward right there! To please my heavenly Father.

According to Jim Rohn, "Resilience is the ability to return to the original form after being bent, stretched or compressed." It's the ability to readily recover from illness, depression or adversity. How would you handle it if you lost everything you had today? What would your next step be? How long would you be depressed and upset and angry? What would it take for you to pull yourself up and start all over again? How resilient are you? Could you learn from all of your disappointments and start all over again?

First, it would take a lot of self-discipline. It would take a lot of positive self-talk to muster up the energy to begin again. It would take a lot of concentration to block out the noise and the clutter of all the negative voices trying to get through, as well as the negative voices of those around you. It would take a lot of discipline to balance the fear and anxiety with the knowledge that, if you did it once, you could do it all over again.

Whether your losses had anything to do with you or not, your future success has everything to do with you. What's happened has happened. You need to get on with your life and begin again. If you lost everything tomorrow and were gathering the courage to try again, it would take self-appreciation. Know in your heart and mind that you have the skills, the talent and the strength to do it one more time. Declare that you can and you will. Believe with all your heart that you can overcome any obstacle, and you will.

Recognize that obstacles are here to help you learn and grow. Rather than be knocked down and put off by your obstacles, shift your perspective. Recognize, as Tony Robbins says, that "Life doesn't happen to you, it happens for you."

Think about it: How do you grow your business and yourself? It's NOT doing the same thing over and over, but instead, it's pushing yourself to the absolute limit. This is when you discover what you're truly capable of and experience the growth you desire. Embrace those obstacles in your life as growth opportunities. Rather than becoming discouraged by them, be encouraged and rise to the challenge!

You can choose to step away from the challenge, or you can choose to face it head-on. It is when we make the choice to break free from our limiting beliefs, to strip away the cloaks of fear that weigh us down, that we create the greatest breakthroughs in our lives, where magic exists and where all our dreams become true possibilities.

Your sense of purpose will pull you through. The best time to know your "why" is before you come face to face with your biggest obstacles. That way, your mission and purpose will help keep you determined to overcome anything that stands in your way.

Sometimes, you must simply take a break and put things into perspective. Right now, you may feel ready to give up, but if you can change your attitude you will see that things aren't as hopeless as you think, no matter how bad they seem. If you persevere with a positive perspective, you will find that things eventually change and you develop a happier lifestyle.

You will experience harsh times as you progress through life, but know that they won't last. When you make it through a difficult obstacle, you will appreciate the good times and the achievements that you earned. Every day in itself is an accomplishment. The bad can be really bad, but the good can be great. Turn every mistake into a lesson. Use the precious time you're given to turn setbacks into stepping stones.

Questions to ask yourself:

1. Do you have unresolved pain from the past? If yes, how are you dealing with it?

2. Is your inner voice congruent with your reality?

3. How resilient are you?

4. Could you learn from all your disappointments and start over again?

CHAPTER 4

People Matter

———⟡———

Self-serving leadership has ramped up in our culture today. Few leaders seem to actually lead from a pure heart. Have you ever worked for leaders who affected people in a negative way? They have no concept about how to deal with people, and at times they lead with an iron fist. There's no grace, no passion, no heart, no character, and people follow only because they feel they have to. Those are clearly positional leaders, and although their leadership styles show in all areas, they hold titles that give them the authority to do things their way. In the meantime, people are being hurt and trampled on without consideration. This is where you see high turnover in many companies; they do not put their people first.

My oldest daughter worked as a manager at a company for a few years, and not once did it seem like the employees mattered to higher management. This company spent much time and money replacing people. It was a frustrating experience for my daughter, to say the least. She finally built up the courage to find a much better job, and she was amazed that she immediately saw a huge difference in the management style at her new company. She was so excited about the idea that all employees mattered and that they received many benefits to keep them happy. She enjoyed going to work and saw herself working there for years to come. Wow! What a difference between companies, and it all depends on leadership.

Unfortunately, many people come from broken places, which have almost always involved other people. The saying is so true: Hurt people keep hurting people. Along those same lines, people who are free, will also free people. The inside of a person always reveals itself to others. This is why it is so important that you and I come from a healed place; a place that I call freedom. We are not bound anymore by pain or adversity; we can now see everything in a new light because we have worked through our stuff. It's the universal law of cause and effect. Whatever you sow, you will reap.

It's not that people intentionally cause pain in others, it's just that they're broken inside and they deal with issues from a broken place and see others with a distorted view. I understand now that I have a responsibility to stay free, so everyone I come in contact with will be blessed and not pained. As leaders, we can look at everyone from the point of view that people are on their own journeys, and we can be intentional in playing a part to help them become better people. This is the powerful legacy we can leave behind for others, by impacting them to see the best in themselves and to reach for higher aspirations. You and I can speak directly into their potential so they can have the confidence to reach it. Having this perspective about people means we take a daily inventory of our intentions and make sure we are walking in integrity with ourselves and with others.

People matter, beginning with you! Caring about yourself first is a must before you can care about others. Loving and respecting yourself in a healthy way will make you whole from the inside out. It's priceless and people will respect you for that. And then your love for others will draw people to you.

As a leader, understand that people are watching a lot more closely than you think. Ask yourself, "Am I doing the right thing in any given situation, for the benefit of everyone?" If a leader cheats, steals or lies, no matter how small it may seem, the leader will lose credibility so fast. It's not worth it in any way, shape or form. Be aware of your actions and intentions in private and in public. Your greatest potential depends on it!

This is why we must improve ourselves daily. Think about the areas where you can improve. One example is arriving on time. I had a friend for years who was one of the neatest people I had ever met.

Our children grew up together. She was entrepreneur-minded, and had a huge heart to serve the Hispanic community; however, in all the years that I knew her, she was never on time for anything. It didn't matter how important an event was, she just couldn't be punctual. I never understood that! A group of women was going to a retreat, and after waiting for her for an hour, we had to leave her behind. It drove the rest of us crazy! She had so many great qualities, but this was one of her biggest downfalls, and no one wanted to partner with her because they couldn't handle her lack of integrity regarding time. Yet, her personality reminded me of Mother Teresa – go figure.

Integrity with people is so important. Also, make every effort to be at peace with others. You definitely can't please everyone and make everyone like you, but you can make the best of every communication opportunity and not leave any gaps which can open the doors to suspicion and doubt. Do your part to be at peace with people as best you know how, shake the dust off your feet, then, at the end of the day, you will feel congruent with yourself and you will sleep well at night.

This is living on purpose. You are the one taking control of your own life, not the other way around. Live out the life of the person you were created to be with all integrity for yourself and for others. It's the greatest gift you can give yourself. When we think about impacting people's lives, we think about impacting them in the grandest ways! We understand that Mother Teresa and Martin Luther King Jr. were influential people who impacted many lives. However, there are countless people with no fame at all doing amazing things that have left huge legacies behind.

This may sound weird, but I like going to funerals. I love to hear the stories of families and friends talking about how the person who passed on left a personal impact on their lives in one way or another. It also amazes me to hear the things that really mattered to their loved ones. It was always the kind word, how they cared and how they loved. It's important to keep on the forefront of what matters in life. No one ever talks about how much money they made and what house they lived in. All of the material stuff is irrelevant at the end of one's life.

You and I have the opportunity to impact someone's life every day. This is when the heart of a leader rises up. It's when you think about others above yourself. Dale Carnegie impacted my life greatly on how to treat people, and it has truly changed my life for the better in many ways. His book, *How to Win Friends and Influence People*, is an excellent book on how to treat people and win favor with them. Isn't that what life is really about – people? Could you imagine what life would be like if we all understood people better? I am a work in progress in this area. It is my greatest desire to do my best and be my best with people and to leave behind a legacy. This is my daily aim. I hope you have this desire, too. Let's end strong! Why not? What do we have to lose? We can make this world a better place. We can lead with heart. This is what really matters.

"If you want to know how to make people shun you and laugh at you behind your back and even despise you, here is the recipe: Never listen to anyone for long. Talk incessantly about yourself. If you have an idea while the other person is talking, don't wait for him or her to finish: bust right in and interrupt in the middle of a sentence." — Dale Carnegie

Even Warren Buffett, one of the most successful investors of the 20th century, took Carnegie's course at age 20. And we have access to all the same lessons in Carnegie's book. We can't make real changes by criticizing people, and we're usually met with resentment, anyway. Remember, when dealing with people, we're not always dealing with creatures of logic, but with creatures of emotion who are motivated by pride and ego.

"Criticism is futile because it puts a person on the defensive and usually makes him strive to justify himself." — Dale Carnegie

Do you know someone you would like to change in some way? When you find yourself getting caught up in other people's annoying habits or behaviors, think of a few reasons why they might be acting the way they are. Say to yourself, "I should forgive them for this because …" and conclude this sentence with an open mind. You'll be in a much better position to hold back from criticizing.

The only way we can get a person to do anything is by giving them what they want. What do most people want? Health, food, sleep, money. Most of these wants are gratified, but there is one longing almost as deep and ingrained as the desire for food or sleep, and it is seldom gratified: the desire to be important. The deepest principle in human nature is the craving to be appreciated. We tend to take the people in our lives for granted so often that we neglect to let them know that we appreciate them. We must be careful to keep in mind the difference between appreciation and flattery, which seldom works with discerning people, as it is shallow, selfish and insincere. Flattery comes from the tongue; appreciation comes from the heart.

Day in and day out, we spend most of our time thinking about ourselves. But if we stop thinking about ourselves for a bit and start thinking about other people's strengths, we wouldn't have to resort to cheap flattery and we could offer honest sincere appreciation.

With words of true appreciation, we have the power to completely change other people's perception of themselves, improve their motivation and be a driving force behind their success. When you think about it like that – when we have nothing to lose and only positive outcomes to gain – why wouldn't we offer genuine appreciation more often?

Next time you're about to give a shallow compliment to someone, stop yourself and offer a few words of honest appreciation instead. For example, instead of commenting about liking your friend's new shoes, tell her that her presentation last week gave you useful takeaways, or mention that you're impressed by her patience when handling tough clients.

If you're worried about coming up with these comments on the spot, make a habit of thinking about people's best features when you interact with them, so that when you see them next, those points will be top of mind.

"Of course, you are interested in what you want. You are eternally interested in it. But no one else is. The rest of us are just like you: we are interested in what we want." — Dale Carnegie

This principle is absolutely key when it comes to influencing others. To convince someone to do something, we have to frame it in terms of what motivates them. And in order to do that, we have to be able to see things from their point of view as well as our own.

Many salespeople spend a lifetime selling without seeing things from the customer's angle, and they wonder why they're not more successful even as they completely ignore the customer's needs. If we can put aside our own thoughts, opinions and wants and truly see things from another person's perspective, we will be able to show them that it is in their best interest to do whatever it is we're after.

"The world is full of people who are grabbing and self-seeking. So the rare individual who unselfishly tries to serve others has an enormous advantage. He has little competition." — Dale Carnegie.

Next time you want to persuade someone to do something, before you speak, pause and ask yourself, "How can I make this person want to do it? How can I frame this in terms of her wants?"

When you're writing an email that contains a request, try replacing "I" and "my" with "you" and "your" as much as possible. Craft your language to make it about them.

When it comes to making friends, we have a lot to learn from dogs. Why do we call them "man's best friend?" Because day after day when we return home, they couldn't be more excited to see us. A dog lives to give love. The same concept applies to humans: We like people who show an interest in us and who admire us. And so, to make people like us, we must show genuine interest in them.

"You can make more friends in two months by becoming interested in other people than you can in two years by trying to get other people interested in you." — Dale Carnegie

If we spend all our time trying to impress people and get them to be interested in us, we'll never have many true, sincere friends. But if, instead, we go out of our way to do things for others – things that require time, energy and unselfishness – and if we greet people with sincere enthusiasm to show them that we are excited to be there with them or talk to them – we will find much more success in cultivating friendships.

Next time you chat with someone, whether a long-time friend or someone you're meeting for the first time, put in the effort to learn things that you don't already know about the person. By asking follow-up questions, you indicate that you're interested in learning more about him or her.

And why do we pay more attention to what we wear on our bodies than what we wear on our faces? Smiling – such a simple act – is very powerful. Of course, it can't be an insincere grin (we all know those are mechanical and we resent them). But a real smile can turn someone's day around. It sends a message of goodwill. It shares hope with someone who is under a lot of pressure from customers, parents or children. Even when we're talking on the phone, our smiles come through in our voices.

"People who smile tend to manage, teach and sell more effectively, and to raise happier children. There's far more information in a smile than a frown. That's why encouragement is a much more effective teaching device than punishment." — James McConnell

Dale Carnegie tells the story of a computer department manager who was desperately trying to recruit a Ph.D. for his department. He finally found the perfect candidate, but the young man also had offers from much larger and better-known companies. When the candidate told the manager that he was choosing to work for his company, the manager asked why. The young man explained: "I think it was because managers in the other companies spoke on the phone in a cold, business-like manner, which made me feel like just another business transaction. Your voice sounded as if you were glad to hear from me … that you really wanted me to be part of your organization." A simple smile can go a long way.

Questions to ask yourself:

1. Are you in integrity with yourself as a leader?

2. Do you really care about people? If not, ask yourself why.

3. What is missing?

4. In what ways are you impacting lives?

5. In what ways can you improve your people skills?

CHAPTER 5

Be Determined

───────※◦◦◦◦◦※───────

To get where we want to be, we must be determined to succeed. There is no way we can accomplish anything major in life without determination. We must have a fire burning inside of us that can never get dimmed by life's circumstances. Is your dream big? Do you think about it all the time? Is it so big that you sometimes assume that you will never accomplish it? If the dream is bigger than you, then you know it is a divine dream. When you can feel the dream and you know that you are supposed to play a big part in it, that's when you take hold of it in your mind and start thinking of ideas for how to make it a reality. One small action, like a simple phone call, can literally excite you to the point of allowing creativity to start flowing. Allow this to nurture your thoughts toward your dreams.

Begin to talk with people you trust who will support your idea. At the same time, be careful who you talk to so you can protect your dream. Remember, not everyone is on your journey with you, and some people will not have the heart to support you or your dream.

And many have not been awakened to realize their own purposes, and for that reason, they will find it difficult to support you. They can give you a hundred reasons why it won't work, and that's not what you need to hear as you are taking a leap of faith to believe that it can work. You want to veer away from any negative comments which can set you back or even crush your dream, because they may lead you to believe in the reasons that it won't work. Negativity can clog your creativity. It's your dream and it's your faith; you have to believe it so much so that nothing or no one will get in the way. This is the kind of determination you will need to push through everything that may come against you in your journey to your destiny.

Get all your ideas out of your head and start writing. Let your ideas run free and start believing and feeling that they will surely come to pass. Your dream is yours to create, and you were created with unique gifts and talents that will only shine brightly through you. How amazing is that? And it's yours for the asking! Are you ready? Do you feel it? Go after it with your full desire and determination.

Work hard to ban your bad habits from putting a halt on accomplishing your dreams. Most of the time you don't realize your bad habits until you are ready to give everything you have to reach your dreams. One of my biggest habits that held me back for a while was that I was busy doing so many things at once that I wasn't accomplishing much. I'm not one to sit down for any length of time; I always have to keep moving, but I still felt like I hadn't accomplished much at the end of the day. Once I decided to get serious about my dreams, I quickly realized that I had to stay focused on one project at a time. I knew that I couldn't allow that day to run me anymore; it was my responsibility to run my day.

I had been a hairstylist for 30 years and I had a full clientele. Every evening that I worked, I would come home hungry and exhausted from being on my feet all day. By the time I ate dinner, all I wanted to do was rest. Well, by this time, it was about 9:00 p.m., and I knew that I had to spend the rest of my waking time with my family before heading off to bed. So trust me, I get it. The days can just go right by and the thought of adding anything extra sounds a bit crazy! But, if our dreams are important to us, then we need to manage our time wisely and set our intentions every day to take the necessary steps to move forward. And most importantly, we have to focus on the results.

Many times I had to get up an hour early and even stay up an hour later, or even make phone calls during my lunch hour. I also kept a book with me that I had been wanting to read. I took a book wherever I went, like the dentist's office, or waiting for my daughter to get out of school. I also contacted and set appointments with the people who I wanted to meet. Whatever it is that you need to do, just set the time and do it, and say no to the things that are not as important. Have the mindset of "No matter what I'm going to accomplish my goals!" Be determined to keep your goals in front of you; keep thinking, visualizing and praying for your dream. And believe like never before that your dream will come to pass.

I know all too well that life's circumstances can hit us so hard at times that we can't even see the near future in front of us. I'll always remember the time I decided to get my certification to be a Life Coach, as I mentioned earlier in this book. It was so exciting for me! I felt like my life was finally going in the right direction. I was still working at the salon and I had saved enough money to go to Texas for the training. Then suddenly, my beloved aunt called and gave me the news that she had cancer. I couldn't believe it! She had always encouraged me and she was my greatest cheerleader. Anytime I accomplished something she would always be happy for me. I knew that she needed me, and I needed her more than ever as I was taking a leap of faith into my passion, my new season, my destiny. Unfortunately, her uterine cancer was painful and aggressive. For the last two months of her life, my family and I would go to spend time with her every evening. This was necessary and beautiful, but it was also exhausting because our lives still had to go on with work and home responsibilities.

During this time I had already set the date to spend a week of training in Texas, and it scared me to think that I would miss her passing or her funeral. I had paid for my training way in advance. And sure enough, my aunt passed away five days before I was supposed to leave for a week, which meant that I would miss her funeral. What was I to do? I had two very important events happening, and I was literally heartbroken because there was no way that I was going to miss my aunt's funeral. I was at a loss. I finally made the decision to go to Texas but to leave the training a day early so I could arrive a little late to my aunt's wake. It seemed like the most logical option to me, so I wouldn't miss either event. I felt bad leaving early that day, and at the same time, I couldn't wait to arrive at the funeral. I have never felt so anxious about being somewhere; my heart was practically pounding out of my chest. I actually arrived two hours late, but at least I was finally there! And it felt great to see my family again during this difficult time.

Challenges that we can't control will come against us at times, and we have to be aware of this fact in advance. We have to know how we are going to handle these difficult situations. I have read many stories of successful people who have gone through tragedies, and they will tell you how they pushed through. This is the big difference between one person who succeeds and one person who doesn't. The choice is yours; you have the power to make decisions that will bring a whole new paradigm shift to your life.

The main principle taught by Napoleon Hill is that whatever the mind can conceive and believe, the mind can achieve – regardless of how many times you have failed in the past, or how lofty your aims and hopes may be. You do this by learning to control and direct your own mind.

Sometimes, when faced with insurmountable challenges, people give in and give up at the precise moment when things are about to change; when success and accomplishment are right there waiting for them to press past the obstacle. You have to be willing to press with all the determination and faith you have inside of you.

According to Tony Robbins, determination is the difference between being stuck and being struck by the lightning power of commitment! Merely "pushing" yourself won't do it; putting yourself in a state of determination will.

Be willing to pay the price. Achieving goals and dreams usually requires a level of sacrifice. It might mean putting everything in life on hold in favor of working toward your dreams, investing all of your savings, or giving up a few hours of sleep each night. Many people proclaim to want to achieve their goals, yet are unwilling to pay the price it takes to make their dreams a reality.

However, before you can choose to pay the price, you must know what the price is. If you don't know what will truly be required to make your dreams a reality, investigate what it will take. Research the costs other people have had to pay to achieve dreams similar to yours. You may even want to interview these individuals to discover the sacrifices they had to make along the way.

You may find that some costs are more than you want to pay. Only you can decide what is right for you and what price you are willing to pay. But if you are willing to pay the price, commit yourself to achieve your dream, no matter what. The willingness to do whatever is required is the magic ingredient that helps you persevere in the face of challenges, setbacks, pain and even personal injuries.

A sense of purpose is built upon the foundation of a higher cause. It defines who you are, where you're going, and who you are seeking to become. With this purpose in mind, you will develop the necessary momentum to overcome anything and everything that stands in the way of you achieving your goals and objectives.

Being successful in life is a challenge. We will all experience failures, but that doesn't mean we should give up. If at this moment you're feeling discouraged, maybe all you need is motivation and determination.

Keep your goal in front of you when you wake up! Keep it in front of you at all times, and stay excited about it. Stay connected to everything related to your goal. It literally takes a lot of thinking, action and planning. Direct your mind to stay in this place. You will stay motivated by constantly taking action. Action is the key to staying in the game. Every day, take action toward your goal and you will see momentum rise. Soon after, you will see results, and that will build more momentum. Push yourself to accomplish short-term goals, one week at a time.

No matter how well you plan and how well you execute your plan, you are bound to meet with disappointments, setbacks and failures along the way to your ultimate triumph. Sometimes, you will encounter what seems like overwhelming odds. At other times, God will test your commitment to the goal you're pursuing.

Adversity is a great teacher. It gives you the opportunity to develop your inner resources of character and courage, and requires that you learn new lessons, develop new parts of yourself and make difficult decisions.

The longer you hang in there, the greater the chance that something will happen in your favor. No matter how hard it seems, the longer you persist – the more likely your success will be.

Your determination greatly depends upon the strength of your desires and how badly you need something, the clarity of your goals, your sense of purpose and your mental attitude. It also depends upon your endurance for pain and suffering and your ability to manage ambiguity and uncertainty. Determined people strengthen their resolve when things are not going in their favor. They may be flexible in their plans but remain focused on their goals until they achieve them. The main quality that will help you to achieve success is your will or your resolve.

Questions to ask yourself:

1. On a scale of 1–10, how determined are you to realize your goal?

2. Do you have people in your life who you trust and who can support your idea?

3. Have you put all of your ideas on paper?

4. What excuses are you making for not taking action on your dream?

CHAPTER 6

Position Yourself

———⟡———

Start where you are and begin today to create success in your life. Drop the excuses, reasons or people to blame, the disempowering attitudes and behaviors, and get on with the business of living the life you know you were born to live. Do what you know you want to do, and do it with passion. Begin today to create the tomorrow you want.

Is your strongest desire to become a heart-driven leader? Be the kind of person who impacts people's lives, no matter where you lead. The number one key is to position yourself in advance. Think about the type of leader you want to become. Examine honestly where you are right now, and write down the areas that you need to work on. Then be intentional and begin working on them. Read books; get a mentor. Read about leaders who you admire and ask yourself why you admire them. What are the qualities that you like about them? Become a lifelong learner. Accept and embrace the fact that everyone has something to teach you. Even in your areas of expertise, remain open to new ideas and ways of doing things.

Position yourself first in your own mind. The way you see yourself shapes the way others see you, and determines how you do everything. People will see you the way you perceive yourself. Believe yourself to be acting in a manner that is consistent with how you feel and who you are – authenticity is essential.

Power positioning is presenting yourself to the right person, at the right time and place, in the right way, with the right message. If you can do that all day long, every day, you will get incredible results.

Position yourself being kind. Be good to yourself and the people you work with and work for. Create the emotional environment around you to be infectious, contagious and advantageous to all who are blessed to be a part of it. Kindness will take you further in success than any other human attribute.

Define what you want for your life and support that vision with energized intention. Know with feeling that this vision of life is yours right now. Follow intention with actions that propel you forward into that life. Read books in different genres; try a new hobby. Let go of resistance and shake up your stagnant thinking.

Simplify your life enough that you don't feel overwhelmed with tasks. Give yourself the time and space to focus intently on what you are doing in the moment. Get into the flow of the activity instead of rushing through it simply to check it off the list. This has been such a breakthrough for me. I didn't realize that I could do a task and stay in the flow. I always thought that I had to feel the struggle to get through a task and that was part of pushing through. And now I just compartmentalize the projects and say an affirmation that everything is being accomplished with ease. Oh my goodness! What a difference it has made in my mindset. I now do my best to do everything with ease.

Your thoughts, feelings, energy and intentions define what you create in your life. This is not some magical power. In fact, the essential ingredient of attracting what you want is old-fashioned action. Combine mental, emotional and spiritual energy with physical action, and you can move mountains.

The values of heart-driven leaders are shaped by their personal beliefs. It's important to examine your core beliefs, as they will become your moral compass. Again, it's about knowing yourself at the core, the values that guide you, because that is how you are going to lead others.

Make it your highest priority to become a person of integrity. You can literally bring people through a transformational process as you guide them to their greatest potential. You can get beyond their weaknesses and see their strengths, and use their strengths so they can shine. Having an honest heart with yourself is of the highest importance when we think about becoming a person of integrity. Guarding your heart at all times is essential when positioning yourself to become a great leader. Always do the right thing because it's the right thing to do. Sometimes it can be the longer route to your ultimate goal, but it will be worth it in the end. Learn from every situation that you come across. Serving as a leader will always give you great lessons from which to learn and grow.

When I first created Women Inspired Network Inc. four years ago, I was so excited! Many women joined the group right away, but within a short time, I learned hard lessons as a leader. Powerful women with different gifts and personalities joined WIN all at once. And to be honest, I wasn't prepared for how to handle certain situations that occurred with some of the women. Nevertheless, I reacted too quickly at times and made rash decisions that caused hard feelings. Unfortunately, some of the women left WIN. Looking back, I know I made stupid mistakes that caused indifference and created disunity in our team.

All it takes is one person to go against the vision and create dysfunction in a team. I have since learned many valuable lessons and studied human relations so that I don't make the same mistake twice.

I have learned to understand other people's perspectives and learn from them. Not everyone is going to think like each other, and it doesn't mean anyone is wrong; they just see things from a different perspective. I am definitely not the same person I was four years ago when I was overzealous about starting my own business and building our community, and running ahead of myself most of the time. Boy, did I have no idea how much I had to learn about leadership.

Now that I'm aware and have continued to learn about people, it has saved me a lot of grief. Now I am enjoying building relationships. It is a beautiful thing when we can enjoy people with different gifts, talents and callings. It makes life interesting. I have committed to always be intentional in growing my leadership skills and continuing to learn lessons about people. Nothing stays the same, so there will always be room for growth as we move forward in our leadership.

Becoming a great listener is a vital skill when leading people to find their needs and desires. Clearly, we can all improve our listening skills. By becoming better listeners, we will improve our productivity and our abilities to influence, persuade and negotiate. What's more, we'll avoid or solve conflicts and misunderstandings. How well we listen has a major impact on our job effectiveness and the quality of our relationships with others.

In addition, it is essential to understanding people. Always listen to understand, before being understood.

We listen to obtain information.

We listen to understand.

We listen for enjoyment.

We listen to learn.

It takes concentration and determination to be an active listener. Old habits are hard to break, and if you have poor listening skills, there's a lot of habit-breaking to do! Be deliberate with your listening and remind yourself frequently that your goal is to truly hear what the other person is saying. Set aside all other thoughts and behaviors and concentrate on the message. Ask questions, reflect and paraphrase to ensure you understand the message. If you don't, then you'll find that what someone says to you and what you hear can be amazingly different!

Also, listen with your eyes. Body language speaks volumes. As you are leading your team, you can visually see if they are committed to your vision. Listening and asking the right questions can make you aware of how well the team is engaged and committed to your vision.

Position yourself to show care and compassion for people. When people know that you truly care, they will follow you and your vision. People follow because they want to, not because they have to. You cannot become a heart-driven leader if you are only thinking about yourself and your leadership position, and not about your team.

Sowing compassion into people's lives will reap incredible benefits for you as a leader, and you will always attract people who want to follow your vision. And what a peaceful place for you to be in, and for those you lead. At the end of the day, there is nothing more gratifying than going to bed with the right heart toward people, knowing you have given your best and served in the best way possible.

You position yourself with your appearance. First impressions get set in stone very quickly. And, like it or not, the way you look is the most important factor in shaping those first and lasting impressions. All you have to do to see that a good appearance is vital is to reflect upon your own reactions to people you meet. Don't you pay more attention to people who look important to you than you do to people who look sloppy? People first judge your importance by the way you look.

You position yourself with your attitude. Some people walk into a room and say, "Here I am!" Others walk into a room and say, "Ah, there you are!" The difference is whether you are self-centered or others-centered; whether you are ego-driven or values-driven. Your attitude toward other people will always show up in the way you treat them. And, more than any other single factor, the way you treat others will determine the way they respond to you.

You position yourself by raising your standards. Define and hold yourself to higher standards to attract high-quality people and situations in your life. To achieve any level of success, you must prepare your mind by deepening your knowledge and sharpening your skill set. The word "cultivates" means to promote, develop or grow something. No matter where you are in your life, you can expand your mind to position yourself for success.

One of the most important steps you can take toward achieving your greatest potential in life is to learn to monitor your attitude and its impact on your work performance, relationships and everyone around you.

We all have a choice. We can choose an inner dialogue of self-encouragement and self-motivation, or we can choose one of self-defeat and self-pity. It's a power we all have. Each of us encounters hard times, hurt feelings, heartaches, and physical and emotional pain.

The key is to realize it's not what happens to us that matters; it's how we choose to respond.

Affirmations repeated several times each day, every day, serve to reprogram your subconscious with positive thinking. An affirmation is made up of words charged with power, conviction and faith. You send a positive response to your subconscious, which accepts whatever you tell it. When done properly, this triggers positive feelings that, in turn, drive action.

Attitude talk is a way to override your past negative programming by erasing or replacing it with a conscious, positive internal voice that helps you face new directions. Your internal conversation – that little voice you listen to all day long – acts like a seed in that it programs your brain and affects your behavior. Take a closer look at what you are saying to yourself.

The ultimate level of human need extends into the spiritual realm. Just as we feed our bodies in response to our primary need to survive physically, we need to feed our spirits because we are spiritual beings. Many people find powerful and positive motivation in their faith. I happen to be one of them.

"Develop an attitude of gratitude, and give thanks for everything that happens to you, knowing that every step forward is a step toward achieving something bigger and better than your current situation." – Brian Tracy

With a positive attitude, you see the bright side of life, become optimistic and expect the best to happen. It is certainly a state of mind that is well worth developing. Surround yourself with positive people. Spend time with people who are positive, supportive and who energize you. If you get too close to a drowning victim, he may take you down with him. It's the same concept when it comes to choosing who to spend your time with. Choose positive people.

Count your blessings. Be grateful and give thanks for the special things in your life rather than taking them for granted. Some people do this by keeping a written journal or posting one special item each day on Facebook. Remember, some of the greatest possessions in life aren't material. Take every opportunity to make a wonderful new memory.

Wouldn't you want more of what you are thankful for? When you are consciously aware of your blessings and are grateful for them, you are focusing more clearly on what you want in your life – and are attracting more of those things. It is hard to be negative about a situation when you are thinking about things for which you are grateful. One of the fastest ways to improve your mood or outlook is to count your blessings.

Gratitude is an attitude. Gratitude is a choice. Gratitude is a habit. When we consciously practice being grateful for the people, situations and resources around us, we begin to attract better relationships and results. The habit will be strengthened as you make the choice each day.

"Who said it could not be done? And what great victories has he to his credit which qualify him to judge others accurately?" — Napoleon Hill

Never underestimate the power of imagination for what you desire. Imagine your dream, believe in it and act on it. Here is a general introduction to the book *The Law of Success* by Napoleon Hill.

Every great railroad and every outstanding financial institution and every mammoth business enterprise and every great invention began in the imagination of some one person.

F. W. Woolworth created the Five and Ten Cent Stores plan in his imagination before it became a reality and made him a multimillionaire.

Thomas A. Edison created sound recorders, movies, the electric light bulb, and scores of other useful inventions, in his own imagination, before they became a reality.

After the Chicago fire, scores of merchants whose stores went up in smoke stood near the smoldering embers of their former places of business, grieving over their loss. Many of them decided to go away to other cities and start over again. In the group was Marshall Field, who saw, in his own imagination, the world's greatest retail store, standing on the same spot where his former store had stood, which was then but a ruined mass of smoking timbers. That store became a reality.

Fortunate is the young man or young woman who learns, early in life, to use imagination, and doubly so in this age of greater opportunity.

Imagination is a faculty of the mind that can be cultivated, developed, extended, and broadened by use. If this were not true, this course on the laws of success never would have been created, because it was first conceived in my imagination, from the mere seed of an idea which was sown by a chance remark of the late Andrew Carnegie.

Wherever you are, whoever you are, whatever you may be following as an occupation, there is room for you to make yourself more useful, and in that manner more productive, by developing and using your imagination. Success in this world is always a matter of individual effort, yet you will only be deceiving yourself if you believe that you can succeed without the cooperation of other people. Success is a matter of individual effort only to the extent that each person must decide, in his or her own mind, what is wanted. This involves the use of imagination. From this point on, achieving success is a matter of skillfully and tactfully inducing others to cooperate.

Questions to ask yourself:

1. What type of leader do you want to become?

2. What are you doing now to position yourself as a great leader?

3. What are your core values?

4. What lessons have you learned so far that are making you a better leader?

CHAPTER 7

Don't Believe In Defeat

As a man thinks, so is he. This is a biblical principle. It's true and proven. Thoughts become things, and if you think defeat, that is the very thing you are going to attract. As I said earlier, my mindset used to be in the mode of thinking negatively in every area of my life. It became a habit for me to think this way. I didn't know any better, so my reality was created by fear, doubt and scarcity. I can't believe how much I sabotaged myself. Living in this defeated state became so unbearable that I began to live a life of torment, and everything I feared came my way. Then moments of depression followed, which I couldn't control. I had no idea at this point of desperation that I could take my mindset back to a healthy state. I didn't realize how much I was damaging my state of mind.

I didn't realize that I had deep-rooted pain in my heart that had allowed my mind to only meditate on negative experiences. From rising in the morning to going to bed at night, my mind was on a one-way street to stinking thinking. I look back now and realize how many years I wasted on negative thinking. Thankfully, it didn't have to end this way for me.

Now, I have transformed the very habits that brought me to this state and I have put them into practice in a positive way. I have a new awareness about life and I can control how I think. I now set my mind to focus only on what is possible for me. I don't believe in defeat anymore. My life is great and getting better every day because my thoughts are directed to everything that is good! What a paradigm shift it has been for me.

I am now conscious of what I think about at every moment. We have the power to control our minds and direct them to think positively. Now I'm not saying that this is easy; no, we have to be intentional. It took a lot of prayer and positive talk and being surrounded by positive people.

I first began to ask myself questions every time a negative thought about myself would come to my mind. I asked, "Is that true about me?" Then I began to think about what I like about myself and what my strengths are. I began to affirm positive things about myself. It felt weird in the beginning, but it has truly changed my life. It has now been a few years since my transformation began. Now that I declare what I want, I have accomplished many goals because I truly believe in myself and my capabilities. Fear and doubt no longer master me. I am definitely in a beautiful state of mind, as I have learned how to control it.

Don't get me wrong; I sure have my moments when I feel the scarcity creeping in and I don't feel fully supported, or confident, for that matter. And there's a slight feeling of desperation inside of me that sometimes reveals itself, and then I get anxious. When I start feeling like this, I quickly remind myself that I have everything it takes to create my dreams and that the right people come into my life at the right time and I am fully supported. I remember how far I have come and I give myself permission to get back up and push hard again, but with ease, not with anxiety. And I remember all the people who fully support me, like my daughters. I have been so blessed by them in so many ways, and their wisdom always brings me a new awakening to move forward on my next journey.

Thankfulness always centers me as well. This journey is definitely about being intentional on a daily basis. No one is going to care about my dream more than me, so I need to encourage myself daily and keep my faith strong, only believing that everything is working out for the best outcome in my life and for those who I impact. My life is full of rich blessings and they're all around me. This is how I remind myself that I am at the right place at the right time and everything is working out as it should. All the lessons that I learn along the way are to grow me and build my character and move me to a higher place. Keeping my mind on what I desire only; not on what I don't desire.

I'm now beyond blessed to be in a beautiful place where I help women break through their fears and become the women they were created to be. I never thought in a million years that I would use my past pain to serve women. I can honestly tell you that when I speak to an audience, it's out of compassion and conviction, to awaken the wounded women and to discover their true identities and purposes so they can break the shackles of fear, torment and pain; so they can bring significance to their lives and to those they lead. My passion explodes for the women to be awakened to their abundance.

We must have the courage to break free! No one can do this for us; we have to rise up on our own. It's time to create your dream and resolve to never go back to the old sabotaging ways. It never served me and it won't ever serve you. Surround yourself with people who don't believe in defeat and who have the greatest positive attitude about life and purpose. This will be life-changing all by itself. Always keep in mind that when you change, everything changes around you. Work on yourself; work on your mindset.

Understand the power of attitude. If you allow negative attitudes (such as anxiety, envy, anger, bitterness or pride) to grab hold of your mind, those attitudes will lead you to make negative decisions that will affect your life in negative ways. But if you choose to develop and maintain positive attitudes, your life will become positive as a result. Even when you encounter the challenges and tragedies of living in a fallen world, you'll be able to deal with them successfully when you choose to approach life with a positive attitude. But keep in mind that changing negative attitudes to positive ones isn't an instant event; I know that full well. It's a lifelong process that requires perseverance. Prayer was my ultimate antidote.

The best solution for you to overcome this defeatist attitude is to take a leap of faith, take that first step, and put yourself in a situation where there is no turning back. You naturally try your best and even if you do fail, it won't matter, because you'll realize that you have gained much more in the very act of doing the task you were most afraid to do from the beginning.

Prepare for obstacles. It's inevitable in this broken world that you'll face difficult circumstances in the future that can lead you to give into negativity if you don't prepare for them now. So invest time in practices that will help you develop new habits of positive thinking that will solidify positive attitudes in your life.

Examine your soul to help you take an honest look inside to identify what specific types of negative attitudes are lurking in there, such as pride, fear, anger, sadness, jealousy, doubt, resentment, bitterness and low self-esteem.

Be accountable for your life. Let go of a victim's attitude, since blaming others for what's happened to you (from divorce to a job loss) won't make your life better. Avoid self-pity and excuses for not changing your life, too. Realize that no matter what has happened to you in the past, you do have the power to change. I know this firsthand.

Listen to audio programs and read powerful books about self-development. And of course, tap into the power of prayer! Go to seminars and continue developing yourself. You will be amazed at the results in a short amount of time. Nothing happens by chance. Faith and a definite purpose will determine your transformation. If you aim at nothing, you will not hit any targets. If I can rise up from the ashes, so can you!

Living a defeated life is torment. You have all the courage it takes in you to rise up! Declare! You don't believe in defeat, you believe in victory! Repeat this as often as you have to until you believe it, then you will soon see your confidence rising up! Now envision the person you want to become and always keep that mental picture in your mind. Do you see it? Now set your goals and go after that dream! That dream that you envision is waiting to reveal itself to you and the world. The real you, with real passions and desires, and real hopes and dreams.

Great ideas and dreams are only ideas and dreams until you commit to taking action on them, and then they come to life. Everything created was first a thought turned into a dream, then a definite action plan. And we all have this ability to create; our Creator imparted us with the ability to create, not compete. We have our own uniqueness. It's all about believing in ourselves.

Repeat affirmations several times each day, every day, to reprogram your subconscious with positive thinking. An affirmation is made up of words charged with power, conviction and faith. You send a positive response to your subconscious, which accepts whatever you tell it. When done properly, this triggers positive feelings that, in turn, drive action. I'll discuss this more in a later chapter.

Fear is a liar and if you struggle with fear and negative thoughts, it's because you believe the lies that fear is telling you. Fear stands for False Evidence Appearing Real. Fear looks and feels true, but it isn't.

Fear says you aren't strong enough, good enough, successful enough, wealthy enough, happy enough, smart enough or talented enough. Well, I say enough with fear! Instead, know the truth. You have everything you need inside of you to be successful. You weren't meant to be average. You have a desire to be great because you were created and born to do great things. You have a purpose. There's a plan for your life. You may be going through a hard time now, but the best is yet to come.

As an entrepreneur, you are definitely going to fail and experience a loss or setback at some point. If it hasn't happened already, it will. That's not to be negative or to discourage you; that's just life. But when it does happen, and when your belief is strong, no failure or setback will have the power to completely wipe you out. Belief in yourself is the name of the game.

If you don't believe strongly in yourself, how can you expect anyone else to believe in you? If you are an employee, you can't expect your boss to fully believe in you if it's clear that you don't believe in yourself. If you are an entrepreneur, you can't expect an investor to believe in your ideas if others can tell that you don't believe in yourself.

The men and women who change the world all understand the incredible power of belief. When you believe you can achieve something, you begin to direct the power of your subconscious mind to help you succeed so that you achieve the outcome you want. So start changing those beliefs today and you'll begin directing your subconscious mind to create more of what you want.

Your personal values, perceptions and attitudes make up your belief system. Self-defeating thoughts are any negative views you hold about yourself and the world around you. Also known as mistaken or faulty beliefs, these views impact your self-esteem, the feelings you carry about your personal abilities and your relationships.

According to Zig Ziglar, to create new beliefs, first you should start working with your thoughts because thoughts lead to beliefs. What you think about all the time – you will eventually believe. You also have to change the way you see things. Because what you see is what you believe. This also means changing the way you see yourself. Because how you see yourself is what you believe about yourself.

People want to be liked by others. However, this desire can become self-defeating when one's self-esteem is tied to the approval of others. A constant need for approval from others can leave one feeling hurt, anxious or angry. The truth is that no matter who you are, not everyone is going to like you. You are a worthwhile person whether or not everyone agrees with you or approves of you.

Your beliefs should help you succeed, not hold you back. If you have a belief that says, "I can't make more money," then that belief doesn't help you make more money. But that belief is what the subconscious mind picks up, and you will actually succumb to the power of your subconscious to make it difficult for you to make money. You may even lose what you have. Instead of directing you to money-making opportunities, your subconscious mind will steer you away from them. So change those beliefs that don't work for you, and start by tracking your thoughts. Self-doubt never disappears. Over time, you just get better at dealing with it.

Ziglar learned that he was the only thing standing between himself and his success. The way he saw himself, the way he saw others, and what he believed about himself and others could either propel his success or inhibit it. He witnessed countless lives changed as a result of the discovery of self-worth. He spent a lifetime encouraging others to believe that they have or can acquire what it takes to achieve their goals.

He became the top salesperson in several organizations before striking out on his own as a motivational speaker and trainer. With a Southern charm and lessons grounded in Christianity, he wrote over two dozen books and amassed a following of millions who were encouraged by his lessons for success.

Norman Van Horne penned this powerful poem about the same concepts:

Power of Thought

When you're gifted with the power of thought

It is a wonderful thing in a way,

But it can also create problems

If your thoughts tend to go astray.

The power of thought brings things to light

That we tend to postpone

But now folks with the power of thoughts

Have today become quite known

So if you possess the power of thought

And don't know how to use it

Consult others who have the same quality,

But very seldom abuse it.

For the Lord gave us the power of thought

To do with as we choose

So hang on to it, always,

It is one power you don't want to lose!

— Norman Van Horne

Fortunately for the human race, we can control our thoughts. We can use our minds and practice the process of thinking. We can make ourselves think thoughts of what we want to be or have.

In 1903, Wallace D. Wattles wrote his book *The Science of Getting Rich*, and a central part of the book is about thinking. To think what you want to think is to think truth, regardless of appearances. To think according to appearances is easy. To think truth regardless of appearances is laborious and requires the expenditure of more power than any other work you have to perform.

We can choose to think as optimists with a positive view of life, or we can choose to think as pessimists. What power our thoughts have!

Regardless of what you do for a living, your real job – the foundation of what you will or won't accomplish – is your attitude. The more upbeat you are, the more likely you are to be successful at whatever you do.

Napoleon Hill spent 25 years in research, analyzing more than 500 of the wealthiest men to find out how they become that way. He came up with the formula that is the subject of his book, *Think and Grow Rich*. Riches, he said, begin with a state of mind, with definiteness of purpose, with little or no hard work. We become what we think about.

Now that we understand the power of our thoughts, we know they can execute any order we direct them to do, and we can use this knowledge to our advantage. By the right application, we indeed can become masters of our destinies.

Overcoming defeat is a crucial aspect of building a life of success and contribution. So many times, people see their lives as sources of despair. Instead, it's time to realize that every obstacle presents us with a question and an invitation to grow.

Overcoming defeat is all about the power to reframe. What we perceive as a problem is actually an opportunity to grow and change. Every obstacle we face carries with it an embedded question. The trick is to find the clarity to ask what each challenge is offering us. Most of the time, we are being invited to stretch and grow. As such, overcoming obstacles eventually teaches us the secret lesson that obstacles, rather than being a source of pain and frustration, are actually our friends and teachers.

So to overcome your obstacles and live the "I don't believe in defeat" philosophy, cultivate a positive-idea pattern. What you do with obstacles is directly determined by your mental attitude. Most obstacles are mental in nature.

If you form the mental attitude that you cannot remove an obstacle, you will not remove it. But when your mind becomes convinced that you can do something about difficulties, astonishing results will begin to happen. All of a sudden, you discover that you have the power you would never have acknowledged in the past.

Obstacles are mental. Norman Vincent Peale told us that while there may be real obstacles in your life, you have to mentally process them, so it is your attitude combined with faith that determines whether or not they stay as permanent obstacles. If you adopt a "through Christ all things are possible" type of attitude, you will tap into a power that will make all things possible!

Questions to ask yourself:

1. What new habits can you create that will keep you out of a defeated mindset?

2. Are there any life changes or patterns that need to happen for you to live in a consistent positive flow?

3. What affirmations can you say out loud that will transform defeated thinking into positive thinking?

4. What are you grateful for?

CHAPTER 8

Branding You

———— ❦ ————

Many people make the mistake of identifying themselves by their business brand. Their persona is about promoting what they do and how they do it. Yet when you meet someone for the first time, your first impression should be about who they are, not their business. This is why it is so crucial to know the best version of yourself. It involves self-discovery, and it takes time to fully understand and get to know who you are authentically and what you're made of. It's a process and you evolve in the journey. Be intentional in learning more about yourself.

Assess your current state. How do people currently perceive you? How large is the gap between the current you and the person you want others to perceive you to be? What needs to change and why? The best version of you is the most authentic you! This is what people buy into; it's you first, then your product or service second. People do business with people who they like. Have you ever asked for the same waiter at a restaurant? Why? Because you like their personality and who they are, and you enjoy talking to them. We all love attractive people, and I'm not just talking about physical appearance. So what makes you attractive? What is unique about you? Leverage your uniqueness; it will benefit you and help you enjoy your work more because you are enjoying the real you. Nothing is more genuine than becoming the person you were born to be. Authenticity is the key. Your personal brand is the sum total of what you do, how you do it and why you do it. It's not something you can fake. It's authentic and deep-seated.

If you get it right, your personal brand will make you stand out from the crowd, shine a spotlight on your expertise and enhance your value. You'll have an energy about you that people can't help but be drawn to. Think about it; no one is like you! Only you can be the best you. But don't make the mistake of thinking your personal brand is all about you. It's not. Your personal brand is not about your work experience or your personal accomplishments. Your personal brand should be about other people; specifically, what you can do for other people.

Instead of focusing solely on your own passions, study the needs of the people in your circles. What are they trying to achieve? What are they struggling with? What are their frustrations? Think about how you could best help these people. Your message should reflect the people you serve, the values that you give and the results you achieve.

Start by asking yourself a few questions: What needs can you address? In what areas can you offer the most value? What makes you different from the rest?

Authenticity is the cornerstone of personal branding. Your authenticity is what allows your audience to trust you, to engage with you and to tell their friends about you. Being authentic is about having stated values and being true to them.

So what are your core values? Include business values, such as driving innovation or personal accountability. You might also add ethical values. Keep your values at the heart of everything you do as you interact with people and network on social media. Wherever and whenever you engage, ensure you do so in a way that shines a light on your values.

Understanding how to brand yourself begins with uncovering your personal brand. Your personal brand is not a tagline or an ad campaign. It's a combination of your interests, beliefs, values, talents, skills and other characteristics. Once you have rolled up your sleeves and dug down deep to find the substance that makes you uniquely you, you're halfway there. Understanding who you are is the jumping-off point for the rest of this process.

Get feedback from those who know you best – at work, at home, anywhere. The true measure of your brand is the reputation others believe about you in their hearts and minds. Notice how they introduce you to others. Ask them what your top brand attributes and core strengths are. If they can easily tell you, then you've succeeded in branding you.

Maintain high standards of honesty with people. Market yourself in the best way you can and let them know what you can do for them. If you discover that you cannot meet their needs, there is always a solution. Point them to someone who has the capability. You will score big for being interested in helping people, and they will come back when you can fulfill their needs.

When you truly own your brand, you don't have to worry about competition because you are true to your brand and you will do things in the way you do them best! Your uniqueness will shine brightly! And you will express yourself and your passion beautifully. You will love life because you love who you are and what you do.

Branding yourself helps to build your business. Further, it helps you form lasting and beneficial relationships with others in professional ways. You will learn more about yourself and others, and above all, you will realize how special and unique you are. This is the best reward!

A leadership brand can help to give you focus. When you clearly identify what you want to be known for, it is easier to let go of the tasks and projects that do not let you deliver on that brand. Instead, you can concentrate on the activities that do. In other words, stay in your lane.

According to Tony Robbins, identity is a set of beliefs and rules that you use to define yourself and that other people use to define you. Your identity influences people more than anything you say ever will. In business, we call this a brand. For example, when you hear someone mention the company Apple, many people think of words like innovative, revolutionary, sophisticated and sleek. A personal brand can also elicit certain words or feelings from others. As for me, I never went into this for the business; I got into this to change lives. When I began, I had no agent and was near bankrupt. Now I am financially free and my work fulfills me. I know my "celebrity brand" opens doors. People already have an opinion about me, whether negative or positive, and there's an energy to it. It allows me to touch more lives. It's the "branding" that allows me to touch lives around the world.

You are a brand and you are in charge of your brand. Your brand is your reputation. It's what you are known for and how people experience you. It's about bringing together who you are, what you do and how you do it.

Personal branding is identifying your assets, characteristics, strengths and skills as an individual. Understanding personal branding will provide advantages in your personal and professional lives. Branding is a mix of how you present yourself and how others see you. It is important to be aware of how you are viewed.

Only you can determine how you want your life to unfold in your brand. You can't control every aspect of your life, but you can create a long-term vision and develop steps to achieve your authentic brand.

This personal brand experience is the opportunity to learn more about yourself so you can identify your uniqueness, skills, strengths and talents. It's your chance to learn about your values and passions, and to find your purpose.

People with strong brands are clear about who they are. They know and maximize their strengths. Now, this is your chance to uncover and define the unique skills that make you stand out from the crowd. As I shared earlier, the two most important days of your life are the day you were born and the day you figure out why. Your branding defines your why and your purpose and adds meaning to everything you do.

When you build your brand, you can make an impact. When you give back to your community, it is an outward expression of your values, passions and purpose, and provides an opportunity to demonstrate your strengths. It's empowering, inspiring and fulfilling for you and those you influence. For example, I love empowering women, and the way I do that is by helping them get unstuck in any areas of their lives. When they experience a breakthrough in a particular area, it is exciting and fulfilling to me at the moment their transformational journey begins. They are now ready to discover their true branding with joy and ease. Oh, the discovery is like a butterfly coming out of her cocoon, and there she is, shining brightly and ready to fly and reach her greatest potential.

Questions to ask yourself:

1. How have you been working on yourself; your true brand?

2. How do people currently perceive you?

3. What is unique about you?

4. Your brand is your reputation; it's what you are known for. What is your brand?

CHAPTER 9

Lead With Meaning And Purpose

⸻ ❧ ⸻

The most important thing for everyone trying to achieve anything worthwhile in life is to understand the "why" before the "what." Know why you do what you do. Strangely, most people don't know why. As I mentioned before, I spent over 25 years not having any clue about my purpose. And I most definitely had no confidence to even attempt to try to discover it.

Once I had the courage to purposely live my life, I soon realized how off-track I was, living a life void of meaning and purpose. My personal and professional lives are now so much richer due to the fact that I live life with intention. When I realized my purpose, I lit a flame of passion in me, and the fire is still burning to this day. Now I fully understand when people talk about the abundant life. I get it now! To discover true meaning in your work, you have to understand why you do what you do. I cannot emphasize that enough, because most people don't.

What is your cause? What is your belief? Why does your business exist? What is your passion? What gives you a righteous anger? Dig deep into your heart and really answer these questions. When you answer them, you will have a clearer picture of how to lead with meaning and purpose.

It will take a lot of thinking and self-discovery to understand your destiny. But without it, you will live without a clear picture and purpose, and never be completely fulfilled. It will become difficult to live or to lead authentically and with confidence. Take your time to ponder these important questions until you fully understand your BIG WHY.

As I have strongly desired and sought to become a heart-driven leader in the past few years, my life has taken an amazing turn for the best. It truly has been transformational in my personal life and as a leader. I realize now that becoming a heart-driven leader is a matter of the heart, because what goes on inside flows to the outside.

This is why it is vital to position yourself right in the beginning. Stay focused on your heart and your purpose. Focus on your priorities and the things that matter most to you, like taking care of yourself and your family. Enjoy those moments of stopping for a bit to smell the roses. We can't forget that at the end of the day, that's what truly matters.

Heart-driven leaders lead with meaning and purpose and values. They build enduring relationships with people. I have been blessed to have built long-lasting relationships with people in my business, and it has been one of the most incredible experiences of my life. I am surrounded by an amazing sisterhood and we have pushed through together. We have created the culture of a safe collaborative where women can let down their hair and share their hearts, as we encourage, support and challenge each other to succeed. And I believe that the strength of the culture comes from our shared core values.

When you lead from the heart, everything flows with meaning and purpose. Creativity and passion will be born, and you will create the destiny that was laid out for you by your Creator.

There is no need to compete with anyone; if you are going to compete, compete with yourself to become better every day. You were created for your destiny. No one in this entire world has the same destiny as you. It is all yours to uniquely fulfill! You were created for your purpose, and you can design your own impact on the world for greatness. Don't be a copycat; that is a scarcity mindset, and the moment you start competing, your creativity will stop and you will focus on someone else's dream. Why look at someone else's dream, when you have your own to create? Become the most creative person in your field, and you will attract the right people. There is so much abundance for everyone. The moment we ask and believe, we will receive. Declare that you will not hold back anymore and go make this world a better place because you are in it!

The moment I decided to lead with meaning and purpose, I began to visualize what I wanted. I began to create, and I am still creating. It has been a transformational journey and I have been loving every bit of it. Never again will I hold myself back and live a life without purpose. I will continue to dream and take risks and become all that I was created to become.

The need for purpose is one of the defining characteristics of human beings. We crave purpose and suffer serious psychological difficulties when we don't have it. Purpose is a fundamental component of a fulfilling life. By focusing our attention externally and giving us a constant source of activity to channel our mental energies into, purpose means that we spend less time immersed in the chatter of our minds – the chatter which often triggers negative thoughts and feelings. Another important factor here is that aligning ourselves to a purpose often makes us less self-centered. We feel a part of something bigger, something outside ourselves, and this makes us less focused on our own worries and anxieties. Our own problems seem less significant when we spend less time thinking about them, so our sense of well-being increases.

Purpose enhances self-esteem. As long as we feel that we are successfully dealing with challenges and moving closer to our goals, our self-confidence increases. We feel a sense of competence and achievement, and an enhanced ability to deal with difficulties and challenges.

So – here's the question: Is the meaning you are giving to your life limiting you or empowering you? Right now, you can choose new, more empowering meanings for your life and create a new world for yourself and those you care about.

According to Tony Robbins: "Is this the end of something wonderful or the beginning of something unpleasant? Are you being punished for your failure or rewarded for your success? The minute you decide to focus on something, you assign it a meaning and infuse it with feeling. How you define an event produces emotion and determines your inner feeling state going forward. The meaning you assign to any event, interaction or outcome defines the emotional tone of your experience and the feelings you generate throughout your life. Meaning equals emotion and emotion equals life. The meaning you give your experiences will always change how you feel – and the emotion you feel always becomes the quality of your life. Our memories are anchors to feeling states, images, sounds and sensations – all of these aspects rely on the meaning we give to them."

Meaning equals emotion; emotion equals life – write this down or memorize it. This is the essence of the entire power of meaning: The meaning you give events, interactions and outcomes determines how you feel. Meaning informs your emotional state. By creating a ladder of positive and empowering meanings, you effectively change the direction of your life and provide yourself with rational, proven reasons why your success will continue.

And it all starts now with your decision to become conscious of the meanings you are constantly creating. This technique is called "reframing," and it's one of the most powerful tools you can use to improve your psychology.

Reframing isn't about pretending a situation is great when it may not be. Rather, it's about discovering what could be great, what you could learn by consequence or how you could use the situation to create a better outcome. Perspective is a powerful thing. When you can reframe a particular experience or interaction, you can often change what happens as a result.

Let's say, for example, your boss is always yelling at you. One way to reframe the situation might be to say, "It's great that she cares enough to tell me how she really feels. She could have just fired me." Or, perhaps you had to pay $2,000 more in income taxes this year. Another way to look at it is, "It's great. I must have made a lot more money."

Human beings tend to attach certain meanings to experiences. We say, "This happened, so it must mean ..." In actuality, there may be an infinite number of ways to interpret any experience. We frame events based on the ways we've decided to perceive similar experiences in the past, forming habitual patterns that we repeat throughout our entire lives. Are your patterns helping or harming you? It's vital to remember that your perceptions are creative – if you define something as negative, that's the message your brain receives and responds to by creating an emotional state to reinforce that reality.

"The quality of your life is the quality of your communication, with yourself as well as with others." — Tony Robbins

Reframing is the difference between being constantly disappointed and being consistently satisfied. By stacking positive interpretations one after the other, you become the author of the success story of your own life. How would you feel at bedtime if every day turned out to be "ideal," "interesting" or even "amazing?" It's closer than you think.

Rick Warren writes in *The Purpose Driven Life*, "Humans were made to have meaning. Without purpose, life is meaningless. A meaningless life is a life without hope or significance. This is a profound statement and one that everyone should spend time pondering. God gives purpose. Purpose gives meaning. Meaning gives hope and significance. There is an awesome truth contained within that logic."

What is your one word that best describes you? That single word may inspire you, focus your attention and help you to understand your why. Where will that one word take you? How does it relate to adding value to others? Why is it significant?

John C. Maxwell, author of *Intentional Living: Choosing a Life That Matters*, wrote, "We all have a longing to be significant, to make a contribution, to be a part of something noble and purposeful." But many people wrongly believe significance is unattainable. They worry that it's too big for them to achieve, or that they must have an amazing idea, be a certain age, have a lot of money or be powerful or famous to make a real difference.

We always remember how people make us feel, not so much who they are or what they do. The reason these leaders are memorable is that they have a sense of their own purpose. But you would be surprised how many leaders today cannot even identify what is important to them.

Many say they don't identify their purpose because they are too busy and they have too much to do. Purpose gives us the stability to stand because when the tough times come (and they will) and the ground beneath us begins to shake (and it will), it is our sense of purpose that keeps us solid. Lead from within: Consider where you are now and where you want to go. See your sense of purpose fill in any gaps between what you are doing today and where you are headed tomorrow.

When I realized my purpose, I discovered that many women struggled with knowing their true identity, and their lack of self-esteem prevented them from truly prospering. It broke my heart to know that there were so many women who suffered from a lack of self-confidence. We were created for a purpose, nothing less, and it is our responsibility to look deep within and discover it. When we finally discover our passion and purpose, everything else will line up for us in amazing ways!

To find your purpose, ask yourself the following questions:

What are my skills, talents, abilities and passions?

What are my values, beliefs and convictions?

What does it look like?

What does it feel like?

What does it sound like?

How do others know what I stand for?

What can they observe in me that shows them my purpose?

When we know our purpose and are able to give and live freely from that space, we also give our best and richest gifts to others. The most important one is the gift of our authentic selves. Know yourself, know your purpose, give freely and pursue the best version of yourself. Get ready to live the life you've always wanted. There is a purpose to everything you do, you just have to have the courage to stop and listen within to understand what it is.

Purpose helps us engage others. When we have a shared mission of something big that inspires others, it is contagious. It builds engagement. People go the extra mile because their minds and (more importantly) their hearts are engaged. This comes from us understanding our personal purpose, sharing it with others and linking it with the work that we do. It also comes from us understanding purpose in others.

Questions to ask yourself:

1. What is your passion?

2. What is your cause?

3. Why does your business exist?

4. What gives you a righteous anger?

CHAPTER 10

A Teachable Spirit

In our leadership journeys, life's lessons are presented to us almost daily in our interactions with people and our big leaps of faith. When we feel stuck in a situation, the value of the lesson is found when we pause, reflect and recognize which process will bring out the best results in the end. We must learn from our mistakes in the past and proceed differently.

I will always remember an important lesson I learned when I took the Dale Carnegie course on human relations. It was one of the best courses I had ever taken, and I was so excited about what I learned! I immediately signed up as a coach for the next course and began to help in the back of the room. There were four of us coaches. One of our roles as coaches was to select those who would receive awards at the end of the course for presenting the best speeches. Every time someone gave a speech, we evaluated it.

Now, during this time my schedule was crazy. I had recently found my purpose and was working and taking courses seven days a week for three months straight. I was also busy at the salon and had just birthed the Women Inspired Network Inc, which took all my remaining energy. I obviously didn't understand time management, but that's another story.

By the time the Dale Carnegie course ran from 6:00 to 9:00 p.m., I honestly had nothing left. I was wiped; so much so that I began losing sleep and not eating well. The stress took its toll on my body and I was diagnosed with shingles. It was horrible! It was one of the most painful experiences I have ever gone through, aside from giving birth. I literally felt my skin bursting with boils. Now you would think that it would've been enough for me to slow down and take a deep breath. But no! How could I miss a class that I was thoroughly enjoying? So there I was, every Tuesday night, barely awake while the students were giving their presentations.

I did not have a good experience as a coach. I should've just graduated and moved on, but I chose to stay. I was too exhausted to pay close attention. The time came at the end of the course when one main winner would receive an award for the highest scores overall. Somehow, I was chosen to give the award. The moment everyone had been waiting for! Here we were, all eyes on me, and lo and behold, I gave the award to the wrong person. I gave the award to the person who was the second runner-up. The coaches in the back room stood up and just stared at me! I knew then that I had made a huge mistake. I couldn't believe it! I failed miserably. I felt horrible. There was nothing I could do. I did everything I could to hold the tears. All I wanted to do was run for dear life, but I knew I had to face this embarrassment somehow.

Soon after, I went to my instructor and burst out crying. I just couldn't take it anymore. I apologized for this huge mistake. I will never forget what he said to me. "What did you learn from this?" His question stunned me because I was expecting him to be so upset and just kick me out for good! I told him that I had been so exhausted for weeks and that I had been working round the clock trying to run the salon business and the network, then I told him how sick I had been as well. I had the shingles at the time, and I was in so much pain, I could actually feel the blisters popping out of my skin at that moment. All I wanted to do was scratch my skin off. It was the worst feeling ever, to say the least.

I grabbed my purse and headed home, and cried like a baby the whole way. I will never forget the deep emotion of frustration and despair. I then made a commitment to myself to never allow myself to ever run on exhaustion as I had done for months. I learned a hard lesson. And now I know it was a lesson well-learned. I have never put myself in that predicament again. Whew! Never again! The saying is true: We live and learn. And that was a lesson learned.

People and circumstances will always teach us something. That's why it's important to give grace, to understand people and their emotions and their actions toward situations. As I think about the Dale Carnegie course, I learned so much about human relations. We truly have to understand people. I know that prior to any personal-development training, I used to just cut people off when I didn't feel supported or connected, or when I was slightly offended. I honestly thought it was the right thing to do. How wrong was I to assume that everyone had to be almost perfect to stay friends, and how imperfect I was in my attitude. I'm grateful that I have been humbled by those experiences, but I have learned and vowed to do my best to value people at all times and in every situation.

Now when I get into a difficult situation, I do my best to see things from the other person's perspective. This has helped me so much because it takes the focus off of me. We all love to be encouraged; however, I now welcome constructive criticism when it comes from the right spirit. It hasn't always been easy to be corrected. Nevertheless, these lessons are stepping stones for learning. My toughest relationships in leadership have been with those who assumed they had it all together. I would think to myself, "Hmm, can I truly be of service to them when they don't think they need anyone's help? On the other hand, I can clearly see how I can help them with the gifts I have been given. I can clearly see their need and what they need to work on."

It's so important to have a desire to listen, learn and apply. We need the hunger to discover what we want and grow through our journeys. We need a willingness to learn, unlearn and relearn. When we stop learning, we stop leading. You will expand if you keep your territory; if you keep expecting and striving to learn. I am determined to always be coachable. As coachable leaders, we need to be consistent seekers. We need to seek growth opportunities from like-minded people and from those who can offer a different perspective. We need to be willing receivers. We need to act upon the feedback that others give us if we are to stay balanced and moving forward.

As a heart-driven leader, I realized that I needed mentors: people who I can model my life after. Mentors have brought life-changing growth to me personally and as a leader. It is now my passion to continue to develop myself and grow in character and competence as a leader in order to build other leaders. I don't believe we are meant to keep everything we learn to ourselves. We are meant to share and to invest in others.

Below are key learnings I've gained from others about being teachable:

Be teachable: Being teachable will open many doors and allow new relationships to build. Learn to love reaching out to people and asking for help; it can be a great blessing. Having this mindset will keep you centered and in a place of humility, especially as a leader. This is where you are authentic and real to yourself and to your team. Surround yourself with people who know more than you do, and keep growing and challenging yourself to become a greater leader. Go to conferences and networking events and meet powerful people in your field of work, and have the courage to ask questions. Always be a student of success!

To be teachable means that you have the mindset of a lifelong learner. You're consistently open to learning from anyone at any time and on any topic. There's no way to escape the fact that being teachable is foundational to growth and character development. Teachability is a choice. We choose whether we are open or closed to new ideas, new experiences, others' ideas, people's feedback and a willingness to change.

The teachable leader will not only humble himself to listen and learn, but when the time comes for him to teach, the first thing he will pour into his students will be the importance of seeking knowledge and wisdom wherever it may be found. When one thinks he has arrived, he has no grasp of how truly distant he is from his destination. Until we're willing to humble ourselves, we're not going to learn anything. To be teachable, we have to first and foremost humble ourselves. We have to become the students. And here's the kicker: The further you go in leadership and the more successful you become, the harder this gets. When you're successful, people think you know more than you actually do. So the combination of being successful and staying teachable is a rare quality in a leader.

Look for and plan teachable moments. If you look for opportunities to learn in every situation, you will expand your talent to its potential. But you can also take another step beyond this and actively seek out and plan teachable moments. You do that by reading books, visiting places that inspire you, attending events that prompt you to pursue change and spending time with people who stretch you and expose you to new experiences. Great leadership requires a teachable spirit.

You see, "teachability," or the ability to be teachable, is essential to your growth as a leader. Humble yourself, study, practice self-reflection and listen to feedback; all of these practices will help you to learn, but they must be willingly embraced. If you do so, you will become a more effective and respected heart-driven leader.

Be deliberate: Being teachable is about being open and willing to be taught and to learn something new. Teachable leaders are deliberate about learning from those around them and they have systems in place which allow them to engage in growth and learning daily. They understand growth and learning does not happen by accident. To remain teachable requires making a daily decision to grow and learn.

People with a teachable spirit approach each day as an opportunity for another learning experience. Their hearts are open. Their minds are alert for something new. Their attitudes are expectant. They know that success has less to do with possessing natural talents and more to do with choosing to learn.

Be humble: How much do we really know, anyway? There is a vast world of knowledge out there. If we acknowledge how little of it we really know, then we can see how much we still have to learn. Always try and be humble, particularly in the moments when you feel compelled to defend yourself to someone.

Accept hardships: Just because someone or something is difficult, doesn't mean it is bad. Successes make us feel good about ourselves but failures help us to become better. The leader who never accepts failure is an unteachable one. If you have made a mistake, learn from it. I often say, "You win some and you learn some." There is no loss in learning. If you learn something from a difficult situation, then it wasn't a loss. Let your hardships teach you.

Have mentors: Find someone who can pour into you. Position yourself as a student. Take notes when someone you respect is talking. They won't mind if you write something down or even ask them to repeat it for future reference. They will be honored that you are listening so closely.

Let go of pride: Leaders who are teachable are people who are willing to admit they do not know everything. If you are to keep growing, you must be prepared to make mistakes. You cannot be prideful and teachable at the same time. To grow, you need to give up your pride. Again, humility is the answer!

To avoid stagnation as a leader, seek out opportunities to listen, learn and apply knowledge not only from like-minded colleagues but also from those who offer different perspectives and even contrary points of view. And don't keep all of the goodness to yourself. Invest in others to multiply the results of your continuous improvement efforts!

Bottom line: If you're not teachable, then you're going to struggle in your leadership role. I rarely get dogmatic in stuff like this, but on this one, I'm pretty darn sure. Teachability is the key to everything good in our lives and leadership.

As a teachable leader, I'm learning things about myself that I must face head-on and then change for the better. I'm sifting out character flaws and inconsistencies that hold my leadership back. At the end of the day, you and I have a choice to make: to choose to be teachable, or not. You are perfectly empowered to live safely and comfortably behind the wall of what you already know. It's totally a choice you're entitled to make. But it's not your only choice. See, the other choice you're empowered to make is to choose to be teachable. Either way, the choice you make comes with a price.

This is even more than the "leaders are readers" truth. A leader who prospers and grows is one who has a teachable spirit. The truth is that your growth determines who you are; who you are determines who you attract; and who you attract determines your success.

Questions to ask yourself:

1. What is one of the major lessons that you have learned in your leadership journey?
2. What has the lesson taught you?
3. How are you doing things differently?
4. Do you have a teachable spirit?

CHAPTER 11

The Big Push!

———— ❧ ————

There will be moments in your journey that feel like nothing is going right. You have been doing all the right things, then suddenly, it feels like you are not getting the support that you once had. You must constantly take inventory of how you are managing your processes. Things need to be shifted at times to keep the momentum, and most importantly, you must understand the situations of the people who are supporting you.

In any way, shape or form, you cannot allow your mind to shift into a negative place that will prevent your dream from coming to pass. You have to believe that it will happen. You have to add faith with a definite purpose and hold on to that, no matter what setbacks occur. Don't ever believe in defeat! There will be times when it will feel like "do or die," and that's when you push like your life depends on it.

I can vividly remember a few times in my career journey when I thought, "If I don't do something now to change a situation, it will affect my business in a drastic way." I can remember at least four crucial moments and I took the risks that would shift the direction of the business. And thank goodness, it all worked out. It's almost like the feeling of a home run in a baseball game: You have to give it all you've got, even if your fingers barely touch the base! The last push will be worth it.

To be honest, sometimes in a split second, I will think, "I'm so tired of pushing, wouldn't it just be easier to get a 9 to 5 job, then go home and not think about anything but dinner and the next day with the same routine?" Then I quickly remind myself of my dreams. I was created for more! I have a purpose! And I need to create value in the most impactful way so that people's lives will be changed. I have to always remember why I'm doing this in the first place. Then and only then will I have the fortitude to climb the next mountain.

No one ever told me that fulfilling my purpose was going to be easy. No successful person will ever tell you that, either. It's all about the courage of not giving up. When it feels like you are at your weakest, that's when you push the hardest and shift things around. You get honest advice from trusted people and take the biggest leap! Many people quit when it gets hard, but declare that you won't! Many will make excuses at this point, but declare that it won't be you! You are now building your faith muscles, which is vital for the steepest climb. Don't quit! It's all waiting for you on the other side of the mountain.

You're almost there! Take a deep breath, pray and believe that you are on your way. All the hard work will pay off big. Give value to others more than ever right now, and let everything that you plant grow a harvest. But, the key is to keep planting and keep planting.

The reason most people never achieve their dreams is that they simply give up. Life was never meant to be easy – it's a constant struggle with extreme lows and extreme highs. Remember that the times when it's most important to persevere are the times that you will be most tested.

"Most of the important things in the world have been accomplished by people who have kept on trying when there seemed to be no hope at all." — Dale Carnegie

Never giving up is a journey with many possible routes and destinations. The strength to succeed is within YOU. You are an example to others, whether you realize it or not. It takes all the courage within you not to give up. Watch what happens along the way. As you move forward, great things will happen. As you stay the course and start to build momentum, you will receive much-needed support that others could write off as luck.

Brian Tracy, a speaker, author and successful businessman, says this about luck: "I found luck is quite predictable. If you want more luck, take more chances. Be more active, show up more often."

The strength to win and succeed is within each and every one of us. We all have the power to win and to be the best people we can be. Sometimes, that strength can be hidden by obstacles or burdens that we face, but it is never lost.

When you persevere, you have the power to change the world. Making an impact may seem difficult, but you are capable of doing so. Changing the world starts with changing YOUR world, which revolves around the people with whom you interact every day. Changing the world starts when you change the environment around you in little and big ways – from smiling at a person to sending a heartfelt thank-you note, to listening to people when they really need to talk to someone. Never giving up is a daily decision that you must make in order to impact yourself and those around you. Think of what our world could be if we never gave up on ourselves or each other.

Speak your vision into existence. When you talk about your goals and dreams, don't talk about what you are going to do, talk about what you are doing to make it happen. Less wishing, more doing.

Want to be an author? First, start writing. Second, when someone asks you what you do, tell them proudly that you are a writer.

It is never too late to get what you want out of life, never too late to be the best you can be, never too late to be successful and never too late to change.

Success is often right around the corner – if only you knew how close you are! If only you knew the impact of one more phone call, one more interview and one more late night working on your passions. Often we give up far too soon. We can't see what the future holds for us, but we sure can keep striving toward our dreams.

I personally think that people stop pursuing their dreams because they want to see, way in advance, what it is all supposed to look like, and when the journey takes a weird turn that they don't understand, they quit. They want certainty in the journey. Don't we all? But, that's not how it works; we can't forget the bumpy roads, the hills and valleys. All these roads are part of the route. We just have to know our next step and trust the journey.

Success is in the journey! Life is in the journey, so let's enjoy it. What would we do otherwise? Live a boring life without a purpose? I've tried that, and it didn't serve me at all. It took me to a place of scarcity and no risks. Now I realize that not taking any risks was the biggest risk I could take. Without risks, I would never know what I was capable of achieving.

When you give it your best shot, you are capable of so much more than you can ever think or imagine! Always focus on staying motivated. Staying motivated makes it hard to fail. Decide to impact people's lives no matter what it takes, and understand why you are doing it. Discover a stick-to-it attitude. Your dreams can get you through even the worst days. If you are struggling, your dreams are your reasons to keep going. They are why you wake up in the morning and try again. They are what make your entire life worth living. Without your dreams, you are nothing.

Crossing the finish line and realizing that you completed your goal will provide an indescribable sense of accomplishment. So, go for it and don't quit because you certainly don't want to miss out on the experience of savoring the success. The road is never easy, but it's worth every turn. Your dreams are only awake if you are. Be careful not to conform to assuming that life will be easier.

The small spark inside of you is trying to get your attention. May you respond and allow it to grow into a flame that will compel you to step into your purpose and change the world around you. Never let that spark die in you – your purpose is birthed from it. And if you allow it to die, you will never fulfill your dream. Your life will always have a deep hole, instead of a life of meaning and purpose.

So, fan the flame and do whatever it takes to get excited about your dream again. It's waiting for you! And when you begin to take action, all the opportunities will be there, because your dream was meant to be created by you. No one is stopping you, but you. Now, buck up! Gird yourself and go make it happen, one action step at a time.

I will always remember meeting a middle-aged woman at a women's retreat where I was speaking, and she had the most somber face. I immediately thought, "This woman is very depressed." She came up to me and asked if she could speak with me. She began to share her whole life with me. She told me how she was a very bright woman who had many opportunities to do something great with her life, but she was afraid to take any risks. She said she would give up and quit a job if she wasn't getting along with a co-worker. Such a sad situation. This woman was healthy and capable of achieving any dream she desired, but she couldn't get past her fears. She was living with much regret and misery. She began to cry and told me that she didn't belong at the retreat and that she should be out there doing something great instead! I was honored to be able to help her to refocus on her dreams and find her confidence.

I'm sure many people live in regret, but the good news is that if you are still breathing, you still have a purpose and it's never too late to achieve it. Get a mentor or coach and push through with support, because that's the journey with no regrets, and it's a much more exciting journey, for sure! Taking risks and believing in yourself allows you to be that person for others.

It has been said that in order for a business to succeed, it must first fail or experience adversity. These struggles help to build fortitude and strengthen the focus. When fortitude is built and focus is strengthened, the synergy creates the perfect formula for business success.

We all have challenges and obstacles in life. And as much as we would prefer that things don't feel or get chaotic, the reality is that they will. But challenges and obstacles are no excuse to give in or give up. Some people think their current circumstances give them a just cause to let go of their dreams or stop moving forward. Not! We don't have that luxury. If we are hungry for success, hungry for a certain way of life, hungry for whatever it is that we desire, then we don't get to make excuses for not moving forward or not continuing on that path.

Have confidence in your abilities. Your confidence may be strong at the start, but it can quickly fade when you encounter obstacles or setbacks. If this happens, remember that you once believed that you had the ability to achieve success. Remind yourself why you felt that way. Don't let what you can't do or what you don't think you're capable of doing stop you from achieving what you want.

Les Brown says, "To achieve something you have never achieved before you must become someone you have never been." That's determination.

Don't wait to be an expert. Start understanding people's problems and then find a way to solve them. Others may know more than you about a particular subject. Who cares? Few people are experts at understanding problems. One thing that successful people do differently is that they don't give up. In the hardest of times, when they are facing a wall, they run into it and break it down. They fight when it's the toughest and, even though they sometimes lose, they rise to another level of confidence which helps with every new challenge.

So what do you do when you hit these tough spots? Start by knowing that you always have options. When one door closes, another door opens. You've got to do your best to stay positive. I've never seen negativity open any doors for people. Negativity almost always closes people off to the world and makes it tough to see options that may be right in front of you. Stay positive!

The only thing that is secure in life is you – your spirit, your heart, your talents and gifts, and your ability to contribute at a high level to something that matters to you. When you live from that knowledge and experience, you'll find (and create) gainful, rewarding work no matter where you go, despite the turbulence around you. And to do that, you need to continually push yourself out of your comfort zone.

Nobody is perfect; don't expect perfection and don't long for it. Let go of that unnecessary pressure. As soon as you accept this, you will find that you will lose the hesitation that has held you back in the past. You will learn to take risks where before you would have run away. With risk comes the chance of failure, but more importantly, the chance of greatness. Failure is a given when you take risks, but the more you can embrace and learn from it, the better off you'll be in the long run. Others notice what you do, whether you realize it or not. People are watching you, and what you do gives them an inspiring role model for growth and change.

Lastly, believe that you are worthy of all that you want to accomplish and you have everything it takes to create it. Believe in yourself, develop yourself and ultimately go create your dream with passion!

Questions to ask yourself:

1. Have you ever felt like giving up on your goals? If yes, what did you do to stay on course?

2. Understanding why you want to accomplish your big goal is important to know. Your "why" will give you the courage to keep going. What is your big why?

3. Do you have a stick-to-it attitude? Why or why not?

4. Do you take risks when opportunities arise? Why or why not?

CHAPTER 12

Manage Your Time Wisely

———— ❧ ————

If you are going to succeed at anything, you must use your time wisely. Have you ever had one of those days when nothing was planned out and you wondered where the day went? Just like that, it was gone!

I have big dreams; some have been accomplished and there are many more waiting to be fulfilled. Every day for years, I would write out my goals. Some would get accomplished and some wouldn't. There are times when I wondered what happened to the day. I wouldn't get much accomplished. Setting goals wasn't the problem; completing them was. It was a struggle for me to accomplish all the tasks I set out to do. I thoroughly defined my goals for the week, but always had the feeling of being behind every time I didn't complete them.

I realized my situation made me feel unfulfilled, because when I tried to enjoy quality time with friends and family, I felt guilty because my goals were not complete. This made me feel unfulfilled because I wasn't present during these precious moments with the people who I loved. I don't know about you, but it's definitely not a good place to be. I wanted to be present in anything that I was doing, but honestly, that wasn't the case most of the time. I then realized that I was not using my time wisely, even though my goals were written out.

If this sounds familiar and you are too busy to accomplish your goals with purpose, then you need to rethink how you are spending your time. Don't let years go by while you feel unfulfilled. Take an honest inventory of your time and figure out what is not working for you.

Distractions and procrastination are killers of success. We can easily get distracted by everything that comes our way. Let's say we have our day planned out and are ready to knock out the list. But 9:00 a.m. comes and a friend calls you and needs to talk, and this call turns into a two-hour discussion. By this time it's 11:00 a.m. Now you realize that it's almost lunchtime, so you stop to eat. And as lunch comes to an end, it's now 12:00, and before you know it, your whole morning flew by just like that! And then comes a strong sense of frustration, because now you realize that time has been wasted and half of your day is gone. More frustration gets stirred up as this scenario plays out day after day. First, we are in no way feeling abundant. This is pure scarcity and these feelings don't produce any strong action or purpose. We realize that life happens to all of us. So, how do we take control of this cycle? I realized that I lacked focus and strategy. I merely made my list, checked some items off, and moved most tasks to the next day. There was no end date or times to complete my goals. What was I thinking? I had no idea how much clarity I lacked when it came to goal-setting.

My daughter Hannah came to me one day and told me how busy and stressed I looked. It was truly an awakening, especially coming from my kid. She was so sweet to tell me the truth, and she told me that she would help plan my weekly goals to make sure I would complete them. I accepted the offer from my little mentor, we worked together, and it was a success. I felt so blessed by her help. Never underestimate who you can learn from. I definitely felt a great sense of relief. The power of time management is vital and priceless because we can't bring back time. My prayer is that I never take life's precious moments for granted. I never want to regret the joys that life brings, and I want to be thankful for all of them. At the end of the day, I want to feel like I have given my best and used my time wisely. This is what matters most to me.

Brian Tracy offers three key time management actions: 1. Get the hard stuff done first. 2. Make a to-do list. 3. Take short breaks. A principle of time management says that hard time pushes out soft time.

This means that hard time, such as working, will push out soft time, such as the time you spend with your family. If you don't get your work done at the office because you don't use your time well, you almost invariably have to rob that time from your family.

As a result, because your family is important to you, you find yourself in a values conflict. There are three key questions that you can ask yourself continually to keep your personal life in balance. The first question is, "What is really important to me?" Whenever you find yourself with too much to do and too little time, stop and ask yourself, "What is it that is really important for me to do in this situation?" Then, make sure that what you are doing is the answer to that question. The second question is, "What are my highest value activities?" In your personal life, this means, "What are the things that I do that give me the greatest pleasure and satisfaction? Of all the things that I could be doing at any one time, what are the things that I could do to add the greatest value to my life?" And the final question for you to ask over and over again is, "What is the most valuable use of my time right now?" Since you can only do one thing at a time, you must constantly organize your life so that you are doing one thing, the most important thing, at every moment.

There are many tools to help you manage your time more effectively so you can put your time to better use. You can make changes which will effectively increase the time you have at your disposal every day. Thinking, planning, finding out how others manage their time, and reading books and articles on time management will develop these skills and give you good ideas.

One easily available change you can make to manage your time is to get up earlier in the morning. Give up watching TV late at night and go to sleep a little earlier than usual. Even waking up only 15 minutes earlier is a great gift of time. It may be a time of solitude before everyone else wakes up, which you can devote to reading, praying, exercising, or planning your day.

To get rid of the feeling that you have too much to do and not enough time, try to feel and think as if you have all the time in the world. This kind of thinking enables you to focus on what you are doing without stress and strain. Always plan your time well and don't waste it on useless activities. Be careful not to procrastinate, and do everything in the best way you can, with focus and attention.

Here is what most women have said to me about time management: "I am so busy helping others achieve their goals, or busy with my family's agenda, that I forget to make time for myself."

As women, we know that we can multitask in many areas; however, it doesn't serve us when we forget about ourselves in the process. Stress sets in, then we are good for nobody! At the end of the day, we did not give it our best. This is something that we have to constantly put in check as we are trying to achieve our goals. We can serve many more in a productive way when we take care of our needs first, and then the needs of those we love and those we serve.

You must know your boundaries and stick to them. Know when you are giving too much of yourself to others. Again, be intentional. Love yourself enough to take care of yourself first. You matter to those who you love and serve. Your busyness can easily sweep you away from the true meaning of life's divine purpose. Living a life of purpose takes a conscious effort on your part. It takes meditation and intention to stay focused. I personally spend time in prayer every morning, and this helps me stay centered and focused before I begin my day.

On your new journey, take time for yourself. I have committed to taking two days off, Fridays and Saturdays, to spend with the people I love. This process has not been easy because I am so used to running ahead of myself with tasks that I need to catch up on. It makes perfect sense to me now to block out time and put my whole schedule in order. And now I also make time for myself and the things I enjoy. I decided to work my butt off from Sunday through Thursday, and now I can finally say that I'm enjoying setting my goals and arranging my schedule. I encourage you to find your own cadence and schedule the time for what matters most in your life.

Questions to ask yourself:

1. How do you manage your time?

2. When you take an honest inventory of your time, what is not working for you?

3. What are your main distractions?

4. Are you clear about your goals?

5. Do you know the steps to take in order to achieve your goals?

CHAPTER 13

How To Build Your Self-Confidence As A Leader

―――――⁂―――――

Here's how to increase your own self-confidence level:

1. Remember, you're not the only one who's afraid.

The only advantage confident-seeming people have is that they're able to take action and project confidence, even if they're feeling terrified inside.

2. Pick a role model.

Choose a leader you admire. What qualities does this person possess? Which of those qualities do you already have, and which do you need to build up? What could you do to develop those qualities in yourself?

3. Take the long view of your career.

What role or position do you eventually want to have? What skills will you need to fill that role? Write them down, and then write down a list of the skills you already have. Make a plan for acquiring the ones you still need.

4. Don't give in to self-doubt.

If you're in a position of leadership or power, that's not an accident. Know that you have what it takes to be there. Others believe in you – prove them right.

5. Own your strengths, as well as your weaknesses.

Are there ways you can turn one of your weaknesses into a strength? Start doing what it takes to make this happen, one small step at a time.

6. Take a good look at your priorities.

You have a lot to do. But do you find yourself getting the low-impact things done first? If so, what are you avoiding, and why?

7. Try something outside the scope of what you've already done.

It could be as simple as making a pitch in a meeting or approaching a prominent person at a business function. If you feel uneasy, remember that's a natural result of stretching your own boundaries. Discomfort equals growth.

8. Take stock of all you do.

Chances are, if you took a few minutes to write down everything you've accomplished in the past week, you'd be pretty impressed with yourself. So do it. Then slip one or two of those accomplishments into your next conversation with a higher-up or customer. Modesty doesn't work in business.

9. Learn to be kind to yourself.

Are you putting unrealistic expectations on yourself? Probably – most of us do. Adjust your own expectations, whether that means changing your timetable for accomplishments or getting others to help. You deserve to treat yourself at least as well as you treat anyone else.

10. Take stock of your greatest strengths.

Select one of them, and think about how you could use it to move yourself and your career to the next level. Make a list of steps you need to take to make that happen, and a plan for when you will take those steps.

11. Trust your own gut.

Your experience, your intelligence and your instincts will lead you where you need to go. So next time you face a challenging situation, get input if you need it, then take decisive action.

12. Give yourself the credit you deserve.

How have you grown in the last six months? And how have you positively changed the lives of other people? Those accomplishments should be celebrated. So celebrate!

Questions to ask yourself:

1. On a scale of 1–10, how confident are you?

2. Do you know your strengths? What are they?

3. Do you need a coach to help you discover why you lack confidence, and to help you discover your life purpose?

4. Is your inner voice congruent with your reality?

CHAPTER 14

Summary

―――❧―――

Lead Yourself First

One of the most important aspects of leadership is to lead yourself, first and foremost. Self-development is vital to successful leadership experiences, and leadership roles will be your greatest teachers. Learn from your mistakes so that you do not keep making the same ones. One of my biggest lessons has been to listen to understand—before I speak. Once I really started working on this, it made a huge difference in my relationships and in my leadership roles.

Learn how to make decisions and stick with them. Indecision is a thief to success, so be clear on what you want and take action. You also must know your purpose and why you are leading. Being a confident leader is vital to your leadership role; you must know your place as a leader so you can be respected by others. Every leader needs a leader to follow, so find a mentor/leader to help guide you in the right direction. Trust the journey; it will not always go as planned, but know that you are at the right place at the right time, and you are growing through difficult situations.

Be in integrity with yourself, do what you say and say what you do, because people are watching a lot my closely than you think. However, there is a peace when you are in your truth. Admit when you are wrong; being vulnerable is a strength. Use your strengths and your uniqueness to lead in your most authentic way and you will be amazed at how people will be attracted to the awesome you! Enjoy this incredible journey. Leadership is about building your character and taking you to higher levels of servitude, which is the greatest honor of leadership. Do unto others as you would want done unto you.

Understanding people and caring for them will make you a leader who will leave a legacy—and that's worth becoming that best leader you can be! You were born for greatness and now you have the opportunity to make others great, too! Leaders create more great leaders. It is an honor to be in a leadership role, and yes, it comes with a price, but the price will be worth it all. Rest assured that it will bring fulfillment in many areas of your life. You lead the most important person in this world—yourself. Everyone wins when the leader gets better. Everything falls and rises with the leadership.

"The quality of your life is the quality of your communication with yourself as well as with others." — Tony Robbins.

Communication is key to the success of a leader. Never leave gaps in any communication; if anything, over-communicate. Otherwise, the topic will be open to doubt and suspicion and ultimately discord in relationships or teams. As a leader, communication builds trust, which is a strong foundation for strong leadership.

People go the extra mile when their minds, and more importantly, their hearts, are engaged. This comes from us understanding our personal purpose, sharing it with others and linking it with the work that we do.

Be intentional with your time management, and remove all the distractions that hinder your goals. Set a time every day that you will take action on your goals, and put your phone away if you have to.

Have a clear understanding of why you want to accomplish your dream goal. Write it out in full detail and read it as often as you can to keep the vision in front of you. Don't allow anything or anyone to get in the way of your big dream. Living in your passion is what will bring fulfillment and meaning to your life.

We all fail in one way or another as leaders, and we learn lessons along the way. But remember that failing is not a reason to give up.

Fail forward. Our failures are lessons for us to learn. This is why it is important to have a mentor or coach to guide each of us in the right direction.

Knowing your purpose as a leader provides clarity, and serves as the trigger for your vision, mission and values. Your vision is what you aspire to achieve; it is the process of becoming. Your mission is what you do; it is the process of doing. Your values are what hold your teams together; they are the foundation for the accountability of the leader and teams. Leaders must work hard to connect the dots between what each individual does and how it enables the teams to succeed.

In closing, here are a few of the most meaningful key points for leaders:

1. Don't criticize or complain about people.
2. Praise improvements, even minor improvements.
3. Give honest and sincere praise and appreciation.
4. Encourage other people to talk and be good, active listeners. Listen to understand before being understood.
5. Be genuinely interested in other people and make them feel important.
6. Be sensitive to people's pride and let them save face.
7. Be respectful of other people's ideas and opinions. Try to see things from their points of view.
8. If you are wrong, be honest and humble enough to admit it.

9. Set a high bar for people and let them know you believe in their abilities to succeed.

10. Have a servant's heart.

Questions to ask yourself:

1. What type of leader do you want to become?
2. What are your clear, defined goals?
3. Who are your mentors?
4. Where do you see yourself five years from now?

About the Author

———— ❧ ————

Sonia Hassey is President and Founder of Women Inspired Network, Inc. and Destiny Women Global, a transformational leadership program empowering thousands of women globally to become heart-driven leaders. Sonia is an exciting speaker whose motivating messages are full of enthusiasm and inspiration. She is on a mission for women to experience their own greatness and to share it with others.

Sonia actively brings heart-centered leadership to her community by supporting women through Destiny Women Global's programs, including community advocacy for young women through her Destiny Women Global Foundation and her Young Women's Leadership Program. Her biggest "Why" is to see women transformed through renewed confidence in their abilities to discover their purpose, believe in themselves, and create the destiny they deserve.

Among Sonia's key programs are the Destiny Women Global Leadership Program, VIP Coaching, Accelerate Coaching, Millionaire Mindset mastermind group, and Team Coaching Program. Sonia's work has significantly transformed women at the personal and organizational levels, as measured by exponential increases in confidence; clarity of direction, goals, and purpose; goal attainment, and increased revenue.

Sonia currently serves on the leadership board of two community organizations. She is the Chief Community Officer of the Hispanic Chamber of Commerce of Contra Costa County and Alameda County, where she leads monthly women's leadership workshops and quarterly women's conferences. Her community work has driven significant community fundraising and has produced support for various local nonprofits. Sonia is a Certified Life Purpose Coach from Dream University, and a Dale Carnegie graduate. She co-authored the book *Catch Your Star*, and is the author of *Butt Naked Leadership* and *Destiny Talks: 20 Brave Conversations with Sonia Hassey*.

Contact Sonia:

Sonia Hassey, President and Founder
Women Inspired Network, Inc.
Destiny Women Global
210 K Street, Sacramento, CA 95816
(209) 329-1783
soniahassey@gmail.com

Engage with Sonia online:

http://DestinyWomenGlobal.com
www.facebook.com/Sonia.Hassey
www.facebook.com/DestinyWomenMovementLeaders/
www.facebook.com/DiscoverBelieveCreate/

Acknowledgments

I dedicate this book to my daughters, Yesenia and Hannah. I thank them for all their support and encouragement during the process of this book and when I started Women Inspired Network Inc. They have seen the successes and struggles in my journey and have always given me wisdom that I have taken to heart. I will always remember these precious moments. I am truly blessed to have them as my daughters. They are both on their own journeys doing what they love, and I am so proud of them. I am forever grateful to them for believing in me. They are definitely my greatest cheerleaders, and I am theirs.

A special thank you to Evodio Walle for believing in me and for all his support and encouragement during the process of writing this book. I realize that I couldn't have done it without him. He gave me the courage and creative ideas to make this book a reality. He also encouraged me to lead the women's initiatives for the Hispanic Chamber of Contra Costa County, which has allowed me to serve many women and increase my influence in many ways.

A huge thank you to a very special friend, Barbara Greer, who has been a great mentor and supporter from the very beginning. Her many encouragements have carried me through some difficult times, and I will always remember them! I am forever grateful.

I want to acknowledge my aunt Maria Garcia, who passed away from cancer. She always believed in me and encouraged me. She always told me, "Sonia, you are going to do great things in life." When she was ill, she would whisper in my ear and tell me how proud she was of me. When she passed away, I felt so lost and I thought to myself, "Who is going to be there for me when this journey gets tough?" I miss her dearly and I will always remember her. She was one brave woman.

And last but not least, a special thank you to all the women who have been through the Destiny Women Global Leadership Program. Together, we've built our confidence and believed that living a life of purpose and integrity is the surest way to lead with excellence. They have trusted me to empower them and to be a part of their transformation process, and now they are all doing amazing things in life and business. Above all, they said yes to their destinies!

I praise God for giving me this special calling that I am so passionate about and for giving me the strength to press through when times were tough. He gave me the confidence that I never thought I had, and revealed my divine purpose to me. The right people came into my life at the right time, and I know that it was no accident. God gave me a vision for women in the beginning, and it is all coming to pass.

www.ingramcontent.com/pod-product-compliance
Lightning Source LLC
Chambersburg PA
CBHW021930190326
41519CB00009B/972